Oxford Discover

Student Book 2

Lesley Koustaff
Susan Rivers

OXFORD
UNIVERSITY PRESS

Scope and Sequence

UNIT	READING	VOCABULARY	GRAMMAR
BIG QUESTION 1	**How are animals different from one another?** Life Science		
1 Page 6	**Amazing Animals** Informational Text (Nonfiction) **Reading Strategy** Compare and Contrast	**Reading text words** *skin, mammals, eggs, amphibians, scales, gills, feathers, wings, fur* **Listening text words** *head, eye, ear, mouth, leg, body* **Word Study** Compound Words	**Subject and Object Pronouns** *Fish* have gills. *They* have gills. Gills help *them* breathe.
2 Page 16	**Leo and Lily's Adventure** Story (Fiction) **Reading Strategy** Compare and Contrast	**Reading text words** *worm, berries, hunt, escape, creep, fight, peck, pinecone, squawk* **Listening text words** *strong, gentle, patient, smart, calm, fierce*	**Adverbs of Frequency** Lily *always* escapes. Lily is *usually* very nervous. Leo *sometimes* tries to catch Lily.
BIG QUESTION 2	**How do things change?** Physical Science		
3 Page 26	**What Is Our World Made Of?** Informational Text (Nonfiction) **Reading Strategy** Cause and Effect	**Reading text words** *flow, solid, liquid, gas, heat, steam, ice, freeze, melt* **Listening text words** *ice pop, balloon, kettle, popcorn, icicle, candle* **Word Study** Nouns and Verbs	**Simple Past of Verb *To Be*** It *was* a liquid. Now it's a gas. They *were* hard. Now they're soft.
4 Page 36	**Let's Make Ice Cream!** Play (Fiction) **Reading Strategy** Cause and Effect	**Reading text words** *cream, sugar, salt, pour, plastic bags, mixture, open, closed, freezer* **Listening text words** *coffee, tea, salad, fruit, vegetables, pasta*	**Simple Past of Verb *To Be*** *Was* the freezer door open? Yes, it *was*. *Were* the students happy? No, they *weren't*.
BIG QUESTION 3	**How are things different now from long ago?**		
5 Page 46	**Then and Now** Informational Text (Nonfiction) **Reading Strategy** Main Idea and Details	**Reading text words** *travel, communication, airplane, news, letter, text message, e-mail, radio, Internet* **Listening text words** *boat, bus, motorcycle, cable car, truck, horse* **Word Study** Words in Alphabetical Order	**Simple Past Regular Verbs** People *listened* to the news on the radio. They *didn't watch* the news on TV.
6 Page 56	**Tell Me a Story, Grandpa** Historical Fiction **Reading Strategy** Sequence of Events	**Reading text words** *arrive, ask, check, enter, poor, crowded, clerk, visit, sick* **Listening text words** *couch, chair, lamp, clock, bathtub, sink*	**Simple Past Regular Verbs** *Did* they *travel* by ship? Yes, they *did*. *Did* they *arrive* in two days? No, they *didn't*.
BIG QUESTION 4	**When do we use subtraction?** Math		
7 Page 68	**Subtraction** Informational Text (Nonfiction) **Reading Strategy** Reread	**Reading text words** *minus sign, subtraction, take away, column, row, test score, single-digit number, double-digit number, left* **Listening text words** *clean, dirty, tired, hungry, thirsty, full* **Word Study** Syllables	**Simple Past Irregular Verbs** Alma *bought* five cookies. She *didn't buy* four. Olivia *gave* her sister twenty stickers. She *didn't give* her twenty-six.
8 Page 76	**Bandar, the Greedy Monkey** Fable **Reading Strategy** Beginning, Middle and End of a Story	**Reading text words** *let go, steal, dig up, hide, jar, greedy, bored, baker, cook* **Listening text words** *knee, nose, foot, arm, face, hand*	**Simple Past Irregular Verbs** *Did* Bandar *go* to a candy store? Yes, he *did*. *Did* he *let go* of the candy? No, he *didn't*.

Billy	Gus	Layla	Dot

LISTENING	SPEAKING	WRITING	WRAP UP
Animal Body Parts Descriptions of different animal body parts **Listening Strategy** Listening for specific information	**Expressing Sympathy** *Are you OK?* *No. My leg hurts.* *Oh, no!*	**Task** Talk and write about favorite animal groups. (Workbook)	• **Review Story** • **Project** Animal Picture Cards • **Review** Units 1 and 2 (Workbook)
Describing Animals Descriptions of animals **Listening Strategy** Listening for details	**Describing an Animal** *Eagles have feathers and wings to help them fly.*	**Pronouns** *Rabbits are very gentle. They are very gentle.* **Task** Talk and write about an animal and what it is like. (Workbook)	
How Things Change Descriptions of changes in states **Listening Strategy** Listening for details	**Accepting a Request** *Please pass the juice.* *Sure. Here you go.* *Thanks.*	**Task** Talk and write about a thing that can change state. (Workbook)	• **Review Story** • **Project** Mixture Book • **Review** Units 3 and 4 (Workbook)
Creating Mixtures Descriptions of food and drink mixtures **Listening Strategy** Listening for specific information	**Describing Food and Ingredients** *Tell me about the party.* *My friends were there. The ice cream was tasty.*	**Contractions** *The ice pops weren't in the freezer. Water isn't a gas.* **Task** Talk and write about a favorite food and drink mixture. (Workbook)	
Social Studies: History			
Life Then and Now An interview with Grandma **Listening Strategy** Listening for specific information	**Asking for Something to Be Repeated** *What country do you come from?* *Would you repeat that, please?*	**Task** Talk and write about something people did long ago but they don't do now. (Workbook)	• **Review Story** • **Project** Interview an Adult • **Review** Units 5 and 6 (Workbook)
In a Museum Children discuss what they are looking at **Listening Strategy** Listening for details	**Describing Travel and Transport** *Where did you travel?* *I traveled to Washington.* *How did you travel there?*	**Adding *–ed* to Some Verbs** *I visited my grandmother. He arrived in New York yesterday.* **Task** Talk and write about traveling to a place 100 years ago and traveling there today. (Workbook)	
Subtraction Problems Subtraction word problems **Listening Strategy** Listening for number details	**Offering** *Would you like some fruit?* *No, thank you. I'm full.* *How about some water?* *Yes, please. I'm thirsty.*	**Task** Talk about and write an interesting subtraction problem. (Workbook)	• **Review Story** • **Project** Subtraction Board Game • **Review** Units 7 and 8 (Workbook)
Number Problems Math problem poems **Listening Strategy** Listening for number details	**Say a Math Problem** *Twenty cows sat in some trees.* *Five fell down and hurt their knees.* *How many cows were left in the trees?*	**Contractions** *Karen doesn't like fruit salad. Bandar didn't let go of the candy.* **Task** Talk and write about three things that were done last night. (Workbook)	

LISTENING	SPEAKING	WRITING	WRAP UP
Social Studies: Community			
Rules in Different Places Descriptions of rules in different places **Listening Strategy** Listening for specific information	**Apologizing** *It's my turn.* *No, it isn't. It's Felix's turn.* *Oh, you're right. I'm sorry.*	**Task** Talk and write about three rules in the home. (Workbook)	• **Review Story** • **Project** Rules Poster • **Review** Units 9 and 10 (Workbook)
Polite or Rude? Dialogues showing different kinds of behavior **Listening Strategy** Listening for specific information	**Being Polite** *Are you using that computer?* *Yes, I am. But we can share.* *Great. Thanks.*	**Subject–Verb Agreement** *He is careful with scissors and glue.* *They were tired yesterday.* **Task** Talk and write about a thoughtful person. (Workbook)	
Clean or Polluted? Descriptions of land and water states and how they affect activities **Listening Strategy** Listening for details	**Reprimanding and Apologizing** *Please don't litter. Use the trash can.* *Sorry. Where is it?* *It's in front of that tree.* *Oh, I see it. Thanks.*	**Task** Talk and write about three natural resources seen every day. (Workbook)	• **Review Story** • **Project** Natural Resource Collage • **Review** Units 11 and 12 (Workbook)
Earth Awareness Week Descriptions of different conservation activities **Listening Strategy** Listening for specific information	**Describing Conservation Activities** *I recycled my milk cartons. Did you?* *Yes, I did. I recycled my milk cartons, too!*	**Verb Tenses to Show Time** *I go to school.* *I'm going to school.* *I went to school.* **Task** Talk and write about something that has been recycled. (Workbook)	
The School Concert Descriptions of different feelings and reactions **Listening Strategy** Listening for details	**Giving Opinions** *Please turn down the music!* *Why?* *I don't like pop music.* *Really? It's my favorite.*	**Task** Talk and write about music and feelings. (Workbook)	• **Review Story** • **Project** Music Mobile • **Review** Units 13 and 14 (Workbook)
Interview with a Pop Star A reporter interviews a pop star **Listening Strategy** Listening for details	**Describing Music and Emotions** *I gave a concert. I was proud. Then I signed autographs. I was excited.* *I played the piano. I was nervous.*	**Using *And* and *But*** *I'm singing and playing the piano.* *Aden is excited, but I'm nervous.* **Task** Talk and write about favorite music and what it sounds like. (Workbook)	
Things We Push and Pull Descriptions of actions that require movement **Listening Strategy** Listening for specific information	**Offering to Help** *Phew! I can't move this. It's too heavy.* *Let me help you.* *Thanks. That would be great!* *No problem.*	**Task** Talk and write about pushing and pulling. (Workbook)	• **Review Story** • **Project** Forces Poster • **Review** Units 15 and 16 (Workbook)
Sport and Movement Descriptions of different sports and actions **Listening Strategy** Listening for details	**Describing Sports** *I run, jump, and throw the ball.* *You're playing basketball.*	**Comparative and Superlative Endings** *Small...smaller...smallest* *Heavy...heavier...heaviest* **Task** Talk and write about speed and movement in a sport. (Workbook)	
Art Class Descriptions of types of art and shapes **Listening Strategy** Listening for details	**Complimenting** *Wow! That's a really great mobile!* *Thank you.* *You're very good at art.* *Thanks. And you're good at math!*	**Task** Talk and write about favorite kinds of art and the shapes used in it. (Workbook)	• **Review Story** • **Project** Art Report • **Review** Units 17 and 18 (Workbook)
Making Art Descriptions of art and art tools **Listening Strategy** Listening for specific information	**Describing Art** *It's a picture of the rainforest. I used green and brown pieces of stone for the trees.* *You made a mosaic.*	**Using Commas in Lists** *My sister bought glue, a box of markers, colored pencils, scissors, and chalk.* **Task** Talk and write about art tools used in art projects. (Workbook)	

Page 190 **WORLD MAP**

In units **1** and **2** you will:

WATCH a video about animals.

LEARN about animal groups.

READ a cat and bird adventure.

WRITE
about what animals are like.

MAKE
animal picture cards.

BIG QUESTION 1

How are animals different from one another?

A Watch the video.

B Look at the picture. What do you see?

1 How many animals can you see?

2 Where do you think they are?

C Think and answer the questions.

1 What animals do you like?

2 Which animals help us?

D Fill out the **Big Question Chart**.

What do you know about animals?
BIG QUESTION Chart

UNIT 1 Get Ready

Words

A Listen and point to the words. Listen again and say the words. 1•02

skin

mammals

eggs

amphibians

scales

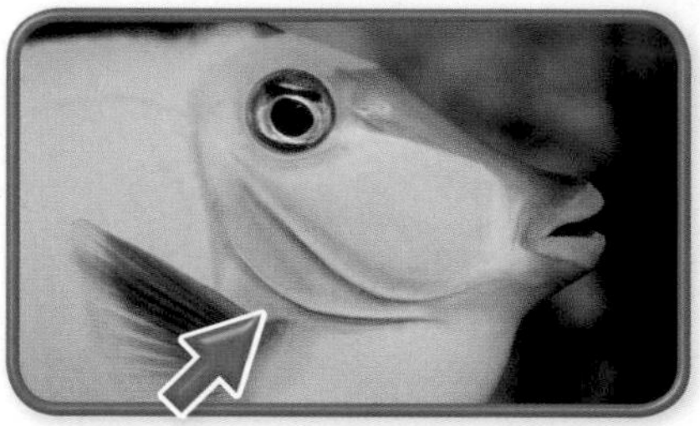

gills

feathers

wings

fur

B Read the sentences. Write the words from **A**.

1 Birds have two of these. Orangutans don't have these. wings

2 Chickens lay these. Some people eat them in the morning. eggs

3 These are all over animals' bodies. feathers fur
scale skings

4 An elephant and an orangutan are part of this group. ______

5 Frogs are part of this group. amphibians

6 Many animals that live in water have these to help them breathe. [illegible]

Before You Read

Think What do you know about fish? Do you like frogs? Why? Why not?

C **Learn** Compare and Contrast

To compare things, we tell how they're the same.
Honeybees and birds both have wings.

To contrast things, we tell how they're different.
Honeybees make hives. Birds make nests.

Read the text. What's the same? What's different? Check (✓) the correct column.

Mice and hamsters are both mammals. They both have fur, four legs, and run fast. Hamsters live inside and mice usually live outside.

Both animals are small.

	Same	Different
1 Fur?	✓	
2 Four legs?	✓	
3 Inside or outside?		✓
4 Big or small?	✓	

D **Look at the title on page 10. What do you think the text is about?**

PREVIEW

Amazing Animals

In this text, we learn about different kinds of animals and the groups they belong to.

This text is an *informational text*. Informational texts tell us about our world.

Life Science

Read 1•03

Amazing

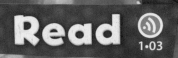

All animals can breathe and move, but they're different in many amazing ways. Here we look at how they are the same and how they are different. This helps us put them into groups.

Birds

All birds have two legs, two wings, and feathers, and most birds can fly. The wings and feathers help them fly and the feathers help keep them warm. Birds lay eggs with hard shells. They keep the baby birds inside safe from animals that want to eat them.

Fish

Fish have gills to help them breathe in water. Scales all over their bodies help keep them safe from dangerous fish that want to bite them. They don't have legs, but their fins and tails help them swim. Fish lay their eggs in water, and their eggs are soft.

Think

How are fish different from birds?

Animals

Amphibians

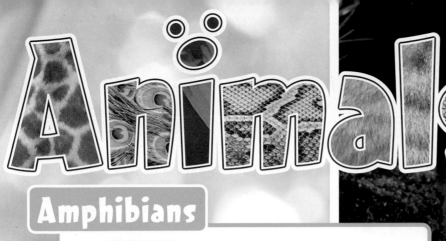

Amphibians are very interesting because they can live on land and in water. Amphibians need to have wet skin, so they live in wet places. They lay their soft eggs in water. They have gills when they're young and the gills help them breathe in water. Most amphibians, like frogs, have legs that help them walk and jump on land.

Think
How are amphibians the same as fish?

Mammals

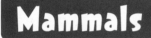

Some mammals live on land and some live in water. Whales are water mammals, and cats, rabbits, and lions are land mammals. Hair or fur covers most land mammals' bodies and this helps keep them warm. People are mammals too! Mammals don't lay eggs. Their babies drink milk from their mothers.

Think
How are mammals different from amphibians?

45secs

Understand

Comprehension

Think **What do you like about the text? Check (✓). Why? Give one reason.**

1 The bird group	☐	☐	☐
2 The fish group	☐	☐	☐
3 The amphibian group	☐	☐	☐
4 The mammal group	☐	☐	☐

A **Ask and answer the question.**

What's your favorite part?

Frogs have wet skin. That's cool!

B **How are birds and fish the same? How are they different? Circle *Same* or *Different*.**

1 How they breathe

Same **Different** (circled)

2 How they lay eggs

Same **Different**

3 What covers their bodies

Same **Different**

4 How they move

Same **Different**

C **Answer the questions.**

1 Where do amphibians live? ~~forest~~ water.

2 How do amphibians move? swim.

3 What do mammals have all over their bodies? fur.

Think **What do you think?**

1 Why can't birds live under water?

2 Why do frogs need to live near water?

Workbook Grammar pages 006–007

Grammar in Use

D **Listen and sing along.** **We Love Animals!** 1•04

Fish have gills to help them breathe.
They have gills to play in the sea!
Birds have wings to help them fly.
They have wings to play in the sky!
Animals! Animals! We love animals!

How do mammals keep warm?
Do you know?
They have fur to play in the snow!
How do amphibians breathe when they swim?
Believe it or not, they use their skin!
Animals! Animals! We love animals!

E **Learn Grammar** **Pronouns**

Fish have gills. They have gills. Gills help them breathe.
Do gills help fish breathe? Yes, gills help them breathe.
How do gills help fish? Gills help them breathe.

What animals have these things? Practice with your partner.

Birds have them.
They're wings.

Communicate

Words

A **Listen and point to the words. Listen again and say the words.** 1•05

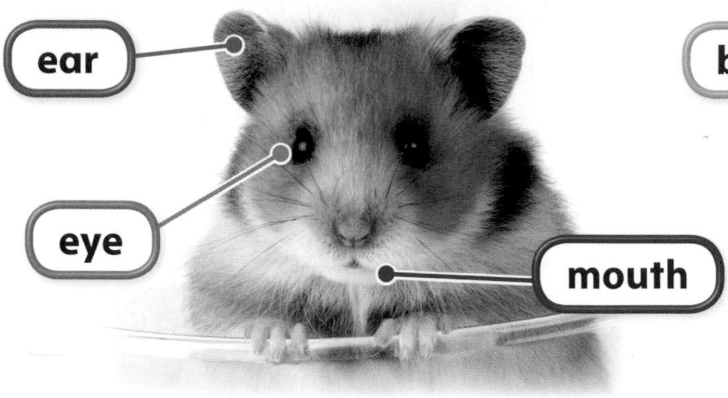

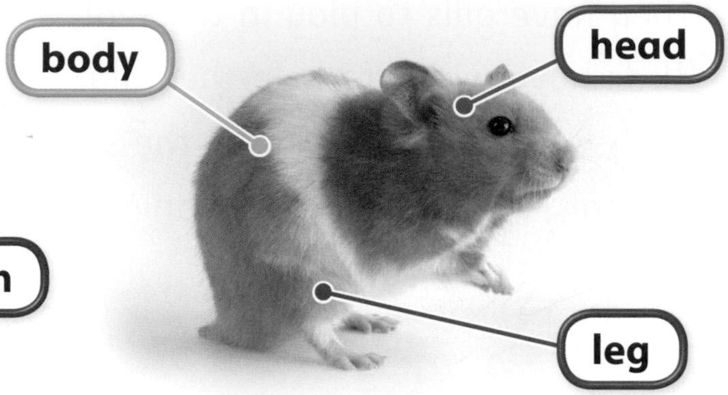

B **Read the clues and write the words.**

1 Some animals have two of these and some have four. legs

2 Eyes, ears, and mouth are on this for most animals. head

3 Most animals have two of these to see with. eye

4 This body part can open and close. Most animals eat with this. mouth

5 Elephants have two big ones but fish don't have any. ear

6 A tiger's legs help move this from place to place. body

Listening

Think **Are fish and bird body parts the same? Why or why not?**

C **Listen. How many of these animals live in the ocean?** 1•06

D **Listen again and circle the correct animal.** 1•07

1 **goldfish / starfish**

2 **cats / rabbits**

3 **whales / elephants**

4 **mice / spiders**

5 **lizards / frogs**

6 **honeybees / eagles**

Speaking

E Listen and repeat. Then practice with a partner. Use the words in the box to help. 1•08

Ouch!
Are you OK?
No. My leg hurts!
Oh, no!

all right
head
ear
That's awful.

Word Study

F **Learn** Compound Words

Compound words are two words put together to make a new word.

star + fish = starfish **honey + bee =** honeybee

Look at the pictures and complete the compound words.

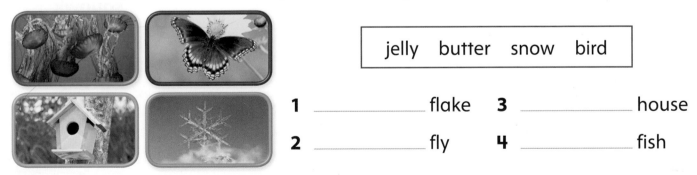

jelly butter snow bird

1 ____________ flake

2 ____________ fly

3 ____________ house

4 ____________ fish

Write Tell your partner three things about your favorite animal group. Now write about them in your **Workbook**. page 09

BIG QUESTION 1

How are animals different from one another?

I think animals belong to different groups.

I think animals have different body parts.

Get Ready

Words

A Listen and point to the words. Listen again and say the words. 1·09

worm

berries

hunt

escape

creep

fight

peck

pinecone

squawk

B Complete the sentences. Write the words.

1 Birds __________ at their food to eat it.

2 A __________ grows on a pine tree.

3 Strawberries are my favorite kind of __________.

4 Some animals in the rainforest __________ for their food.

5 The dog and the cat don't like each other. They often __________.

6 A __________ is a long, thin animal. It lives underground.

7 Bobby's pet bird can __________ out of the window.

8 Cats can __________ very quietly. Other animals can't hear them coming.

9 Birds can __________ loudly. It's a funny sound!

Before You Read

Think How can animals help people?
Do you help at home?

C **Learn** Compare and Contrast

Remember, to **compare** things, we tell how they're the same. To **contrast** things, we tell how they're different.

Read the text. What's the same? What's different? Write the words in the Venn diagram.

Hugo and Ivan are ten years old. Hugo lives in a big house in the country and Ivan lives in a small apartment in the city. They both have pets. Hugo has a big dog and Ivan has a small goldfish.

Hugo
1 big house
2 big dog

Both
1 ten years old
2 have pet

Ivan
1 small apartment
2 gold fish (small)

D **Look at the title and pictures on pages 18–19. Guess the things that happen.**

Leo and Lily's Adventure

In this story we read about the adventure of a cat, Leo, and a bird, Lily.

This story is an *adventure story*. Adventure stories are usually exciting because a lot of things happen.

Read 1•10

Leo and Lily's Adventure

Leo and Lily live in a big garden near a forest. Lily is red and yellow. She's friendly, but she is usually very nervous. Lily flies from tree to tree in the garden and she hops in the grass. She eats worms, nuts, and berries. Leo is black and white. He is very fast and very clever. He's brave, too. He climbs trees in the garden and he hunts for mice … and birds! Leo sometimes tries to catch Lily, but Lily always escapes. Leo can run fast, but Lily can fly. This makes Leo angry!

Think

How is Leo different from Lily?

Think

How are Leo and Lily the same?

One day, Leo sees Lily in the garden. Leo wants to catch Lily. He creeps through the garden very slowly and quietly. But Lily sees Leo and she flies away into the forest. Leo chases Lily. Lily flies and flies and Leo runs and runs. Soon they are a long way from the garden and they don't know the way home. It's dark in the forest. Leo and Lily are scared.

Leo and Lily hear a noise. It's a fox! The fox is hungry. It wants some dinner. It wants to eat Leo! Leo tries to fight the fox, but the fox is very big.

Lily is in a tree. She pecks a pinecone. The pinecone falls and hits the fox on the head! Leo escapes and climbs up the tree. The fox is angry. It can't climb trees.

Leo and Lily wait in the tree for a long time. At last, the fox goes away. Leo and Lily are safe, but they want to go home now. Lily flies up very high. She sees the garden! She squawks happily. Lily shows Leo the way home. But Lily is small and her wings are tired. She sits on Leo's back and Leo carries Lily home.

Leo and Lily are safe at home in their garden again. They're friends now. Lily flies around the garden and Leo never tries to catch her … Well, hardly ever!

Understand

Comprehension

Think **What do you like about the story? Check (✓). Why? Give one reason.**

			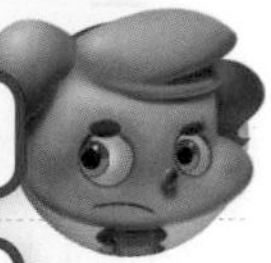
1 Why Leo and Lily don't like each other	☐	☐	☐
2 Their adventure in the woods	☐	☐	☐
3 How Leo escapes from the fox	☐	☐	☐
4 Why Leo and Lily are friends at the end	☐	☐	☐

A **Ask and answer the question.**

What's your favorite part?

Lily pecks the pinecone. It's funny!

B **Compare and contrast Leo and Lily. Write the words in the Venn diagram.**

- can fly
- scared
- clever
- can run
- friendly

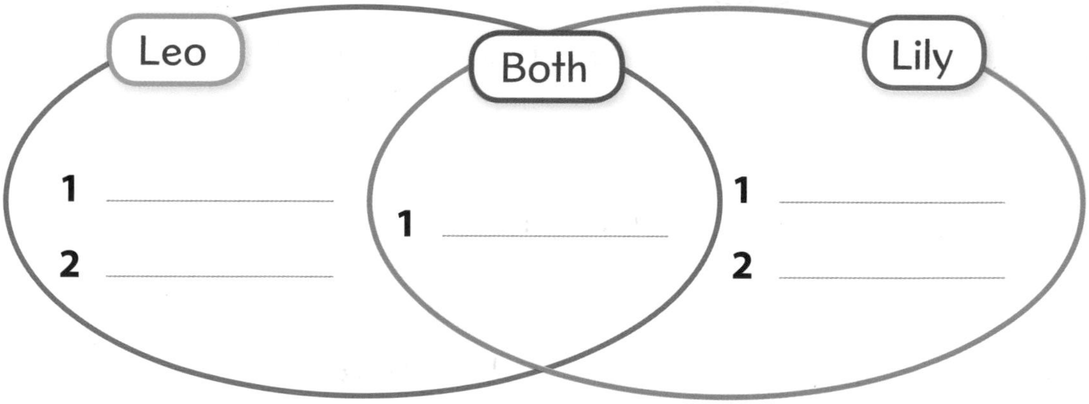

C **Number the events in the correct order.**

☐ Leo tries to fight the fox.

☐ Leo and Lily wait in a tree.

1 Leo chases Lily.

☐ Lily shows Leo the way home.

Think **What do you think?**

1 Which animals can be pets?

2 Can animals help each other?

Workbook Grammar pages 014–015

Grammar in Use

D Listen and sing along. **Cats and Birds** 1-11

Meow! Squawk! Meow! Squawk!
My cat and bird always fight.
They never get along together.
And fighting isn't right.

Meow! Squawk! Meow! Squawk!
I hardly ever sleep at night.
Why can't my cat and bird be friends
And treat each other right?

Meow! Squawk! Meow! Squawk!
I usually have to shout.
I sometimes say they must be friends
Or I won't let them out!

E **Learn Grammar** Adverbs of Frequency

Lily always escapes.	always ✓✓✓✓
Lily is usually very nervous.	usually ✓✓✓
Leo sometimes tries to catch Lily.	sometimes ✓✓
Leo hardly ever tries to catch Lily now.	hardly ever ✓
Leo and Lily never fight now.	never X

Practice with your partner.

Me	Name ...
I always ...	He / She always ...
I usually ...	He / She usually ...
I sometimes ...	He / She sometimes ...
I hardly ever ...	He / She hardly ever ...
I never ...	He / She never ...

F Now tell the class about your partner.

I always eat ice cream in the summer.

He sometimes watches TV in the evening.

Communicate

Words

A Listen and point to the words. Listen again and say the words. 1•12

strong

gentle

patient

smart

calm

fierce

B Circle the correct answer.

1 An elephant can be big and strong. True False

2 A lion is always gentle and calm. True False

3 A dog can be fierce and patient. True False

4 A monkey can be smart. True False

5 A mouse is always strong and fierce. True False

Listening

Think What animals do you think are smart? Why?

C Listen. Where are the children? 1•13

D Listen again and check (✓) the correct animal. 1•14

1

2

3

4

Speaking

E **Describe an animal. Your partner tells you the animal group it belongs to. Use the words in the boxes to help.** 1•15

Writing Study

F **Learn** Pronouns

Some words can take the place of nouns.
These words are called pronouns.

Rabbits are very gentle. They are very gentle.

Write the pronouns for the underlined words.

1 My friends and I are playing. ______

2 The dog is barking at Tom. ______

3 The drums are very loud. ______

4 The city is dangerous. ______

5 Lions can be fierce. ______

Write **Tell your partner about an animal that you know. Say what it is like. Now go to your Workbook and write about it.** page 17

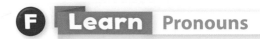

Wrap Up

A Listen and read along. 1•16

The students are learning about animal groups.
Billy, come here and tell us about your pet.
Billy's pet is a fish.
Wonderful!
Boo doesn't have legs but she has fins. She's very smart!
Layla's pet is an amphibian.
Lovely!
Toby has big eyes. He has gills like Boo and is always very calm.
Dot's pet kitten is a mammal.
Interesting!
This is Charlie. He has beautiful white fur. He's very strong!
Gus's pet is a bird.
Amazing!
Eddie has beautiful feathers. He likes to fly around my room.
Zak has a pet lizard.
Help! Run!
Lizzy is usually gentle, but sometimes she's fierce!

Project: Make Animal Picture Cards

B **Make animal picture cards.**

- Draw or find a picture of one animal for each card.
- Write the name of the animal below the picture.
- Write three facts about the animal group on the back of the card.

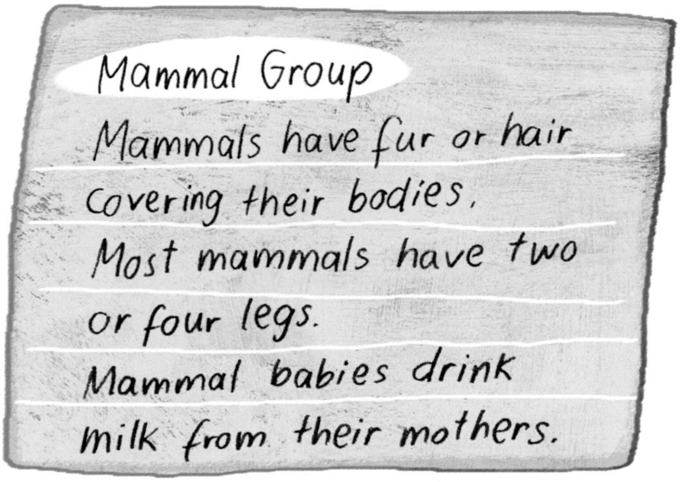

Mammal Group
Mammals have fur or hair covering their bodies.
Most mammals have two or four legs.
Mammal babies drink milk from their mothers.

C **Put your Animal Picture Cards on the wall. Tell the class about an animal.**

D **Play a game with your partners. Place your Picture Cards picture-side down on a desk. Partners read the sentences on the backs of the picture cards and guess the animals.**

This is a rabbit. Rabbits have fur all over their bodies.

BIG QUESTION 1

How are animals different from one another?

A **Watch the video.**

B **Think more about the Big Question.**

C **Complete the Big Question Chart.**

What did you learn about how animals are different?

In units **3** and **4** you will:

WATCH a video about how things change.

LEARN about what things are made of.

READ about how to make ice cream.

WRITE
about things that can change.

MAKE
a book about mixtures.

BIG QUESTION 2

How do things change?

A **Watch the video.**

B **Look at the picture. What do you see?**

1 What is the weather like?

2 Where do you think this is?

C **Think and answer the questions.**

1 What things change?

2 Can you hold water in your hand?

D **Fill out the Big Question Chart.**

What do you know about how things change?

UNIT 3 Get Ready

Words

A Listen and point to the words. Listen again and say the words. 1•17

flow

solid

liquid

gas

heat

steam

ice

freeze

melt

B Write the correct words to complete the sentences.

1	Water is a ______________.	liquid / solid
2	We put ______________ in drinks to make them cold.	gas / ice
3	On a hot day, ice cream can ______________.	melt / freeze
4	We can't hold a ______________ in our hands.	solid / gas
5	We ______________ cold water to make it hot.	freeze / heat
6	Water in a river can ______________ over stones.	melt / flow
7	A book is a ______________.	gas / solid
8	You can see ______________ on very hot water.	steam / ice
9	On a very cold day water can ______________.	freeze / melt

Before You Read

Think **Are there any liquids in your backpack? What solids are in your kitchen at home?**

C **Learn** Cause and Effect

Cause and **effect** tells how one event makes another event happen.

A **cause** is why something happens.

The **effect** is what happens after the cause.

Cause	Effect
I water the plants.	They grow.
The ice cream is in the sun.	It melts.

Read the sentences. Match the causes and effects.

In the winter, it's sometimes cool and rainy. When it's very cold, it snows. When there's a lot of snow, children don't go to school. They stay home and they're happy. In winter, there's often ice on the streets, and sometimes people slip and fall.

Cause

1 It's very cold.
2 There's a lot of snow.
3 Children stay home.
4 There's often ice on the streets.

Effect

a Sometimes people fall.
b It snows.
c Children don't go to school.
d They're happy.

D **Look at the pictures on pages 30 – 31. What do you think the text is about?**

ice liquid
solit

PREVIEW

What is our World made of?

In this text, we learn about what things are made of.

This text is an *informational text*. Remember, informational texts tell us about our world.

Physical Science

Read 1·18

What is our World made of?

Everything in our world comes in three different states: solid, liquid, or gas.

Solids

We can see and feel solids. Some solids are hard, and some solids are soft. Trees and feathers are solids. You're a solid, too!

Liquids

A liquid is a thing that can flow. Some liquids are thick, and some liquids are thin. Juice and milkshakes are liquids. Can you think of other kinds of liquid?

Gases

The air that you breathe is a gas. We can't usually see a gas but sometimes we can feel it when it moves. On a windy day, we can feel the wind on our bodies.

Things can change from one state to another when we make them hot or cold.

When we make water very cold, it freezes and changes to ice.

When ice or snow heats up, it melts and changes back to water.

When we heat water, it boils and changes to steam.

Look at these three pictures of things changing from one state to another.

The snow was a solid and now it's a liquid.

Think

What's the cause of the snow melting? What's the effect?

The water was a liquid and now it's a solid.

Think

What's the cause of the water freezing? What's the effect?

The water was a liquid and now it's a gas.

Think

What's the cause of the water boiling? What's the effect?

Understand

Comprehension

Think **What do you like about the text? Check (✓). Why? Give one reason.**

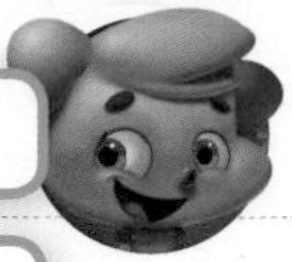 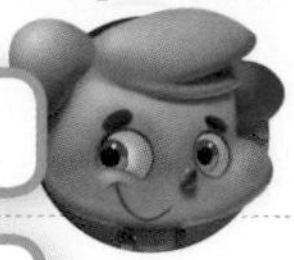 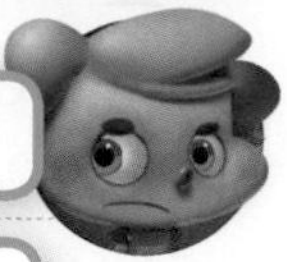

1 Solids	☐	☐	☐
2 Liquids	☐	☐	☐
3 Gases	☐	☐	☐

A **Ask and answer the question.**

What's your favorite part?

Water can change to a solid or a gas. It's interesting.

B **Match the causes and effects.**

Cause	Effect
1 Water freezes.	**a** It melts.
2 We heat ice.	**b** It changes to ice.
3 Water boils.	**c** It changes to steam.

C **Complete the statements.**

1 We can see and feel this. It can be hard or soft. This is a ___solid___.

2 This flows. It can be thick or thin. It's a ________.

3 We cannot usually see this. Sometimes we can feel it. It's a ________.

Think **What do you think?**

1 Why do we boil liquids?

2 Can all solids change to liquids?

Workbook Grammar pages 024–025

Grammar in Use

D **Listen and sing along.** **The Snowman** 1•19

This was my snowman.
My wonderful snowman.
But now he's melting away!
His name was Joe, my man of snow,
And now he's melting away!

Those were his black eyes,
And that was his red nose,
But now he's melting away!
He wasn't small, he was very tall,
And now he's melting away!

E **Learn Grammar** **Simple Past of Verb *To Be***

It was a liquid. Now it's a gas.

They were hard. Now they're soft.

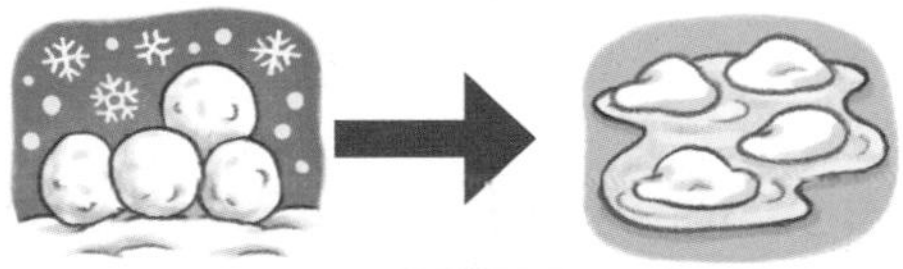

What was it then? What is it now? Practice with your partner.

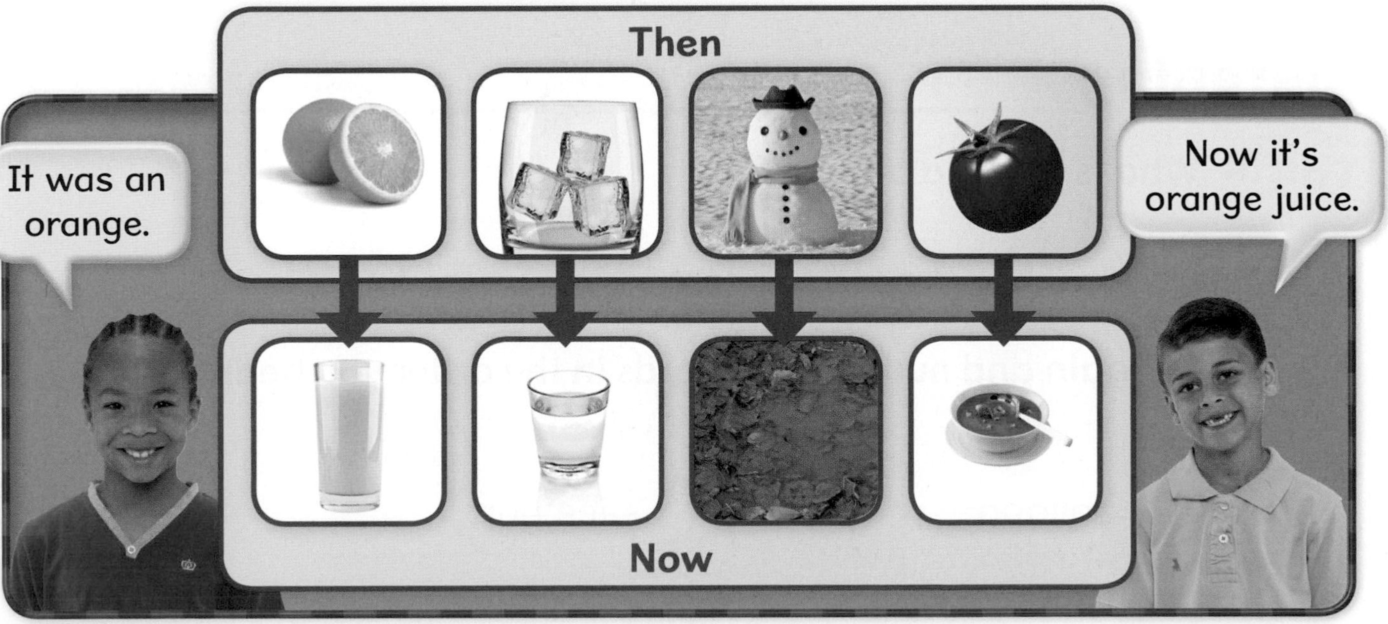

Then
It was an orange.
Now it's orange juice.
Now

F **Look around the classroom. Find something that has changed from one thing to another. Tell your partner about it.**

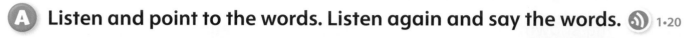

Communicate

Words

A **Listen and point to the words. Listen again and say the words.** 1•20

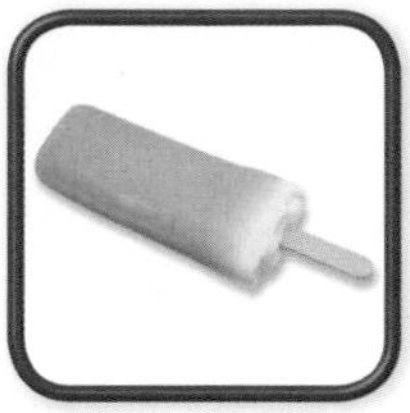
ice pop

balloon

kettle

popcorn

icicle

candle

B **Read the clues. Write the word.**

1 People think I'm fun to play with. If I get too big, I pop! What am I? balloon

2 I help people heat water for drinks. What am I? ______

3 I can grow on a house when it's very cold outside. What am I? ______

4 I get noisy when people make me hot. People eat me. What am I? ______

5 People use me to see in the dark. Be careful! I'm hot. What am I? ______

6 I'm very cold and people eat me on a hot summer day. What am I? ______

Listening

Think **What's inside a balloon?**

C **Listen. What happens to popcorn?** 1•21

D **Listen again and number the words in the order you hear them.** 1•22

a	☐	balloon	d	1	ice pop
b	☐	icicle	e	☐	kettle
c	☐	candle	f	☐	popcorn

Speaking

E **Listen and repeat. Then practice with your partner. Use the words in the box to help.** 1•23

chips
cookie
OK.
Of course.
No problem.

Word Study

F **Learn** Nouns and Verbs

Remember, some words can be nouns *and* verbs.

Noun: **Steam is a gas.**

Verb: **She steams the carrots.**

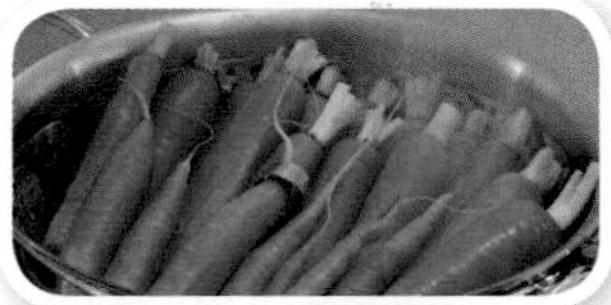

Read the sentence. Write the word.

1 Look! The eagle chicks can fly !

2 My friend and I ________ video games together.

3 We ________ at the pond in the summer.

play

fish

fly

Write **Tell your partner about a thing that can change state. Write about it in your Workbook.** page 27

BIG QUESTION 2

How do things change?

I think solids can become liquids.
I think liquids can become gas.

UNIT 4 Get Ready

Words

A Listen and point to the words. Listen again and say the words. 1•24

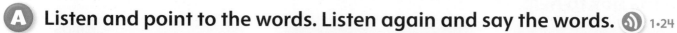

cream

sugar

salt

pour

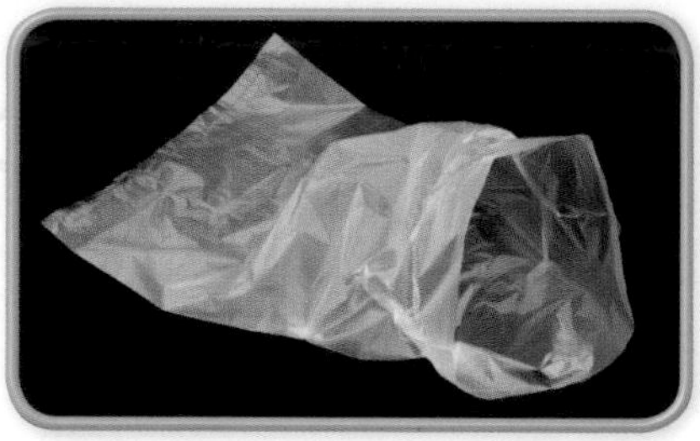

plastic bags

mixture

open

closed

freezer

B Look at **A** and write the words.

1 Food: ____salt____ ____________ ____________

2 Things in a kitchen: ____________ ____________ ____________

C Complete the sentences. Write the words from **A**.

1 I ____________ the milk into the mixture to make a milkshake.

2 When the door is ____________ I can see outside.

3 When the window is ____________ I feel hot.

Before You Read

Think Do you like ice cream? Do you have parties with your friends?

D **Learn** Cause and Effect

Remember, a cause is why something happens. The effect is what happens after the cause.

Read the causes. Write the effects.

Omar feels awful. He's really cold. His mother heats some water and makes him some lemon tea. Omar drinks the tea and feels warm. He takes a short nap and when he wakes up he's hungry! His mother heats water in a pot, and puts in some chicken, carrots, and onions. Omar eats the soup and feels good again!

Cause	Effect
1 Omar is really cold.	His mother makes him tea.
2 Omar drinks the tea.	
3 He's hungry.	
4 Omar eats the soup.	

E **In the story, students make something that is cold and sweet. What do you think it is?**

PREVIEW

Let's Make Ice Cream!

This story is a *play*. A play is acted on a stage by actors.

Read 1•25

Let's Make Ice Cream!

Ms. Woods
Grade 3 teacher

Luis

Judy

Mark

Students

Mr. Jenkins
Science teacher

Ms. Woods: Today is our school party. Let's go to the cafeteria and get the ice cream you bought yesterday. It's in the freezer.

Students: Oh, no! It's liquid!

Luis: Yuck!

Judy: That was our ice cream!

Mark: Was the freezer door open?

Think
What is the cause of the ice cream melting?

Ms. Woods: Yes, it was. It was open all night. Now there's no ice cream for the party.

Think
What is the effect of the ice cream melting?

Mr. Jenkins: What's wrong? Why's everyone so sad?

Ms. Woods: It was our job to bring the ice cream for the party, but it melted. Now we can't have ice cream.

Mr. Jenkins: Sure you can! You can make ice cream. I can teach you!

Students: Yippee!

Mr. Jenkins: OK, kids. Get big and small plastic bags, cream, sugar, vanilla, and salt. Then come to my classroom.

Students: Ready, Mr. Jenkins!

Mr. Jenkins: My freezer was closed all night, so I have ice. Now, let's make ice cream.

Students: Yes! Let's make ice cream!

Mr. Jenkins: Mix the sugar and vanilla and cream.

Students: Mix the sugar and vanilla and cream. Done!

Mr. Jenkins: Pour the cream, sugar, and vanilla mixture into the small bag.

Students: Pour the cream, sugar and vanilla mixture into the small bag. Done!

Mr. Jenkins: Put the salt and the ice cubes into the big bag.

Students: Put the salt and the ice cubes into the big bag. Done!

Mr. Jenkins: Now put the small bag in the big bag.

Students: Put the small bag in the big bag. Done!

Mr. Jenkins: Now shake, shake, shake! What do you have?

Luis: Hey! Look! We have ice cream! And we didn't use a freezer!

Think
What is the effect of shaking the mixture?

Students: How is the ice cream, Mr. Jenkins?

Mr. Jenkins: It's great! Can I have some more?

Comprehension

Think **What do you like about the play? Check (✓). Why? Give one reason.**

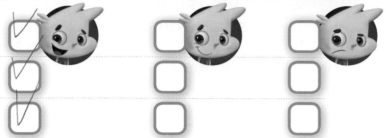

1 Mr. Jenkins helps the students.	✓	☐	☐
2 The students make ice cream.	✓	☐	☐
3 People eat the ice cream.	✓	☐	☐

A **Ask and answer the question.**

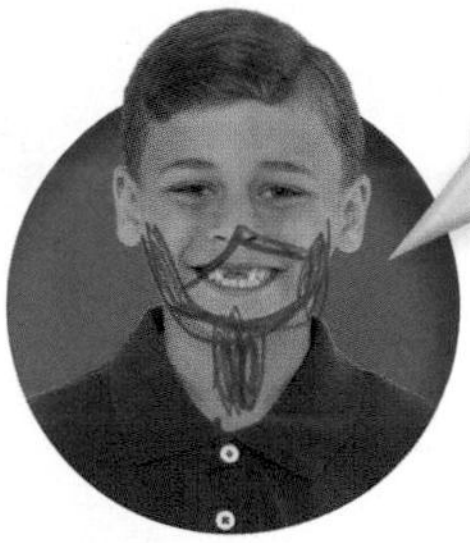

What's your favorite part?

The students make ice cream. I like ice cream.

B **Read the causes. Write the effects.**

Cause	Effect
1 The freezer door was open all night.	a The ice cream melted.
2 The students don't have ice cream.	b They can't eat
3 They make ice cream.	c They cab party

C **Read the sentences. Circle the correct answer.**

1 The students need to bring fruit to the party. True **False**

2 The students pour the mixture into a bag. **True** False

3 The ice cream wasn't good. True **False**

Think **What do you think?**

1 Why did Mr. Jenkins help the students? LOLIPOP

2 What was fun about this school party?

Grammar in Use

D **Listen and sing along.** **Making Ice Cream** 1•26

Where were you yesterday?
We were at a party.
It was fun to make ice cream
With all our friends!

Was the ice cream in the freezer?
No! It was quick to make.
Was the ice cream in a bag?
Yes! Shake, shake, shake!

Where were you yesterday?
We were at a party.
It was fun to make ice cream
With all our friends!

E **Learn Grammar** **Simple Past of Verb *To Be***

Was the freezer door open? Yes, it was.
Were the students happy? No, they weren't.
Where was the ice cream? It was in the freezer.

Ask your partner questions about the picture. Use the words in the box.

ice cream door window books students

F **Think of a mixture. What things are in it? Ask your partner.**

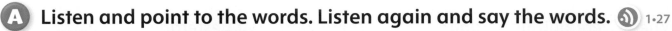

Communicate

Words

A Listen and point to the words. Listen again and say the words. 1•27

coffee

tea

salad

fruit

vegetables

pasta

B Think about the words in **A** and add them to the chart.

We wash ...	We don't wash ...
1 salad	1
2	2
3	3

Listening

Think What foods do you like to mix?

C Listen. What liquids and solids do we heat? 1•28

D Listen again and check (✓) the ingredients you hear. Then circle the correct food. 1•29

1
- [x] water
- [ ] oranges
- [ ] milk
- [ ] juice

fruit / **tea**

2
- [ ] cucumbers
- [ ] tomato
- [ ] sausage
- [ ] avocado

salad / **coffee**

3
- [ ] tomatoes
- [ ] carrots
- [ ] sausages
- [ ] onions

vegetables / **pasta**

Speaking

E **Take turns to ask your partner about the school party, yesterday.** 1•30

Tell me about the party.
My friends were there. The ice cream was tasty. The games were fun.
It was ...
They were ...

Writing Study

F **Learn** Contractions

Remember, contractions are two words joined together. We make contractions by taking away a letter and adding an apostrophe (').

is + not = isn't	**was + not = wasn't**
are + not = aren't	**were + not = weren't**

Read the sentence. Write the contraction.

1 The ice pops weren't in the freezer. (were not)

2 Water isn't a gas. (is not)

3 Coffee and tea aren't solids. (are not)

4 The refrigerator wasn't on all night. (was not)

Write **Tell your partner one of your favorite foods. Is it a mixture? Now write about it in your Workbook.** page 35

Wrap Up

A Listen and read along. 1•31

Let's make dinner. We can have pasta, vegetables, fruit, and cream.
And ice pops!
Billy and Dot start to make dinner. Gus puts the food away.
Put the ice pops in the freezer, Gus. And heat the water, please, Dot.
Look at the water!
It's steam. It was a liquid and now it's a gas! Cool!
Where are the vegetables?
They're in the water. Now it's soup!
Dot looks for the cream but the cream was in the freezer.
Look! Ice cream. It was a liquid and now it's a solid! Cool!
The ice pops!
The ice pops weren't in the freezer.
Oh, no, Gus!
Uh-oh! They were solids and now they're a liquid! Sorry!

Project: Make a Mixture Book

B **Write about three food mixtures.**

- Draw or find pictures.
- Write sentences about the mixtures.

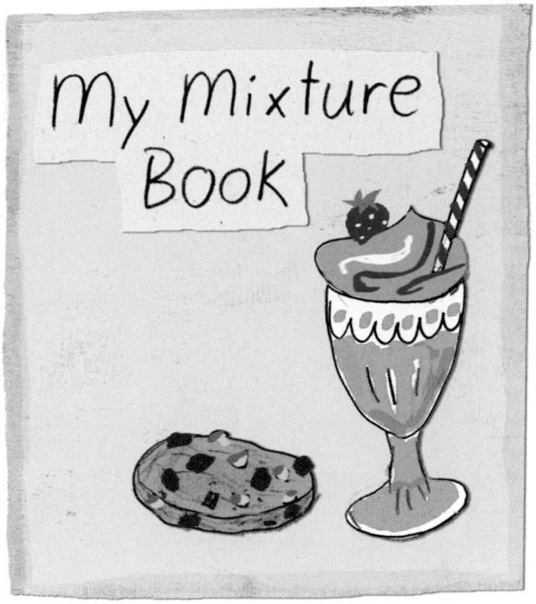

C **Display your Mixture Book. Tell the class about one of the mixtures in your book.**

This is soup. It's a mixture of solids and liquid.

This is vegetable soup.
It's a mixture.
It's liquid.
It also has solid things in it.

D **Walk around the room. Look at the books. Choose your favorite mixture. Say why it's your favorite.**

Ice cream is a mixture of cream, fruit, and ice. I like it!

BIG QUESTION 2

How do things change?

A **Watch the video.**

B **Think more about the Big Question.**

C **Complete the Big Question Chart.**

What did you learn about how things change?

In units **5** and **6** you will:

WATCH a video about things now and long ago.

LEARN about things now and long ago.

READ a story about a man who came to New York.

WRITE about something people did long ago.

MAKE a report about an interview.

BIG QUESTION 3

How are things different now from long ago?

A Watch the video.

B Look at the picture. What do you see?

1 How did people travel then?

2 Why were there so many people?

C Think and answer the questions.

1 Did your grandmother have a cell phone when she was young?

2 Are you the same now as you were three years ago?

D Fill out the **Big Question Chart**.

What do you know about how things now are different from long ago?

Get Ready

Words

A Listen and point to the words. Listen again and say the words. 1•32

travel

communication

airplane

news

letter

text message

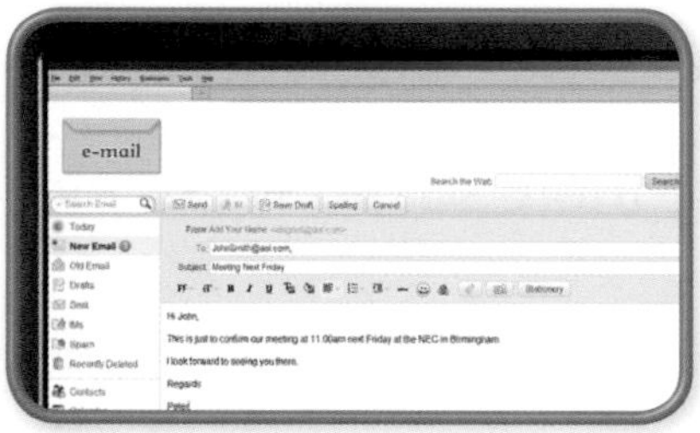

e-mail

radio

Internet

B Read the sentences. Write the words.

1. We fly on this to go somewhere far away. airplane
2. We can send these to our friends. ________ ________ ________
3. We listen to this to hear songs or news. ________
4. This is something you do if you like to go to new places. ________
5. E-mail and text messages are examples of this. ________
6. This is something we use a lot to find information. ________
7. We can turn on the TV or listen to the radio to hear this. ________

Before You Read

Think How do you get to school? Can your grandparents use the Internet?

C **Learn** Main Idea and Details

The main idea is what a text is about. There is one main idea. Other sentences in the text tell us more about the main idea. These are called details.

My neighborhood was very different long ago. There was a big farm, and it was quiet and safe. There weren't a lot of buildings or people. It's different now.

- My neighborhood was very different long ago.
  - There was a big farm.
  - There weren't a lot of buildings or people.
  - It was quiet and safe.

Write the main idea and details.

Ali was different a long time ago. He was a naughty little boy. Now he's a good student. He was always late for school. Now he's always early.

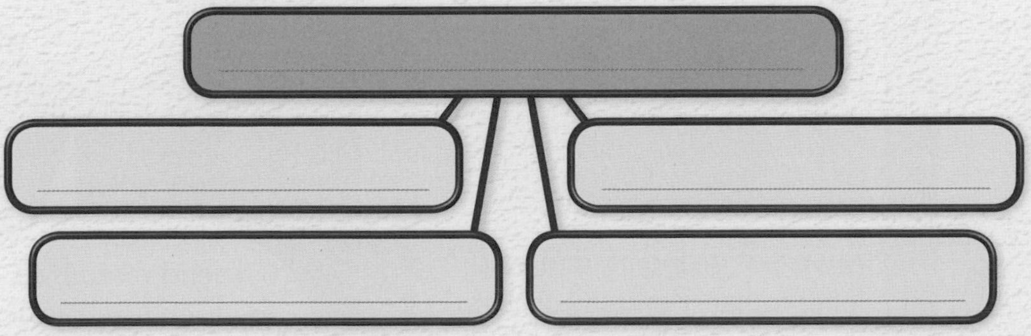

D Look at the title on page 50. What do you think the text is about.

PREVIEW

Then and Now

This text is an *informational text*. It is on a website. Remember, informational texts tell us about our world.

Social Studies: History

Read 1•33

Then and Now

Today, communication and travel are fast, and it's easy to get news. But a long time ago, things were very different.

Think
What's the main idea?

Communication

Long ago, people used letters to communicate. They mailed letters to friends and families. Letters were carried by horse and cart, and later by train or boat. Today, communication is different and letters are carried by airplane. We can use e-mail, text messages, or phone calls to communicate quickly with friends and family all over the world.

Think
Find one detail of the main idea.

From Mary-Lou
Posting a Letter
My great-grandma mailed a letter to her friend in London. It took two months to get there.
I send e-mails to my friend in London. She can read them right away.

News

Before newspapers, people talked to each other to get news. Then people printed the news on paper and newspapers started. Later they listened to the radio for news. Today we can get news any time we want.

They listened to news on the radio at 6 o'clock every day.

They watch the news on TV and read it on the Internet anytime they want.

Travel »

People long ago walked from place to place or traveled by horse and cart. When they traveled long distances they went by train or ship. It was slow and difficult. Today we can travel in cars, fast trains, buses, or airplanes to go to places that are far way. We can travel to places across the ocean or across the world in a day. Travel is fast and easy now.

People traveled for two days from New York to Boston.

Fast Ticket

It takes 30 minutes to travel from New York to Boston today.

How do you communicate with your friends and family?

Understand

Comprehension

Think What do you like about the text? Check (✓). Why? Give one reason.

1 Communication	☐	☐	☐
2 News	☐	☐	☐
3 Travel	☐	☐	☐

A Ask and answer the question.

What's your favorite part?

Travel long ago was slow and difficult. I'm glad we have planes now.

B Write the main idea of the text and three details.

Main Idea

____

Communication	Travel	News
______________	______________	______________

C Number the events in the correct order.

☐ People listened to the radio for news.

☐ People watch TV or read the news on the Internet.

1 People talked to other each other to get news.

☐ Newspapers started.

Think What do you think?

1 Long ago, people didn't usually go to places very far away. Why not?

2 How does a letter get from Australia to Egypt today?

Workbook Grammar pages 042–043

Grammar in Use

D **Listen and sing along.** **Great Grandma** 1•34

Great Grandma traveled on a ship,
The trip was long and slow.
She moved here from a different land,
Many years ago.

Great Grandma walked from place
to place,
In sun or rain or snow.
She didn't use a car or bus,
Many years ago.

Great Grandma listened to the news,
On her old radio.
People didn't watch TV,
Many years ago.

E **Learn Grammar** **Simple Past Regular Verbs**

People listen<u>ed</u> to the news on the radio.
They didn't watch the news on TV.
People travel<u>ed</u> by horse and cart.
They didn't travel by airplane.

What did you do last night? Write three things. Then tell your partner.

watch > watched	play > played	clean > cleaned	talk > talked

I cleaned my room.

Me
1
2
3

I didn't clean my room. I talked to my friend.

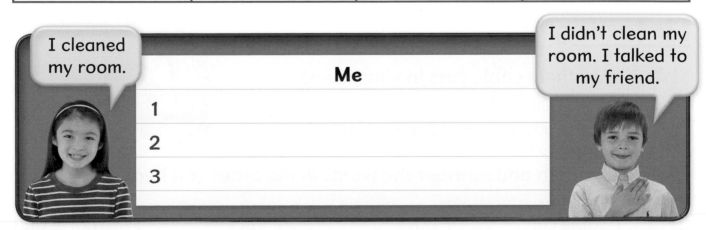

F **Tell your partner something you didn't do last night.**

Communicate

Words

A Listen and point to the words. Listen again and say the words. 1•35

boat

bus

motorcycle

cable car

truck

horse

B Think about the words in **A** and add them to the chart.

A lot of people can travel on these at the same time.	Only one or two people can travel on these at the same time.
1 bus	1
2	2
3	3

Listening

Think Are there cable cars in your town?

C Listen. Who has a new motorcycle? 1•36

D Listen again and number the words in the order you hear them. 1•37

- [ ] cable car
- [ ] bus
- [1] truck
- [ ] horse and cart
- [ ] boat
- [ ] bicycle
- [ ] airplane
- [ ] motorcycle

Speaking

E **Listen and repeat. Then practice with a partner. Use the words in the box to help.** 1-38

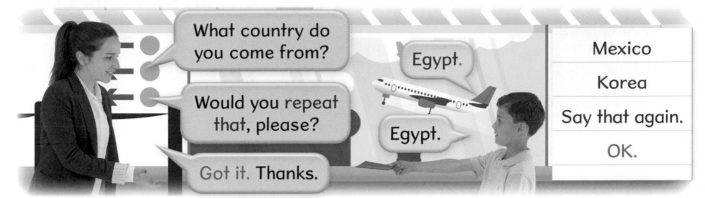

What country do you come from?
Egypt.
Would you repeat that, please?
Egypt.
Got it. Thanks.

Mexico
Korea
Say that again.
OK.

Word Study

F **Learn** Words in Alphabetical Order

Words in a dictionary are in alphabetical order. These three words all have the same first letter. Look at the second letters. They are in alphabetical order. If they're the same, too, we look at the third letter.

bark
boat
bus

Number the words in alphabetical order.

a		b		c	
☐	apartment	☐	closed	☐	steam
1	amphibian	☐	cream	☐	stop
☐	animal	☐	coyote	☐	statue

Write **Tell your partner about something people did long ago but they don't do now. Now write about it in your Workbook.** page 45

BIG QUESTION 3

How are things different now from long ago?

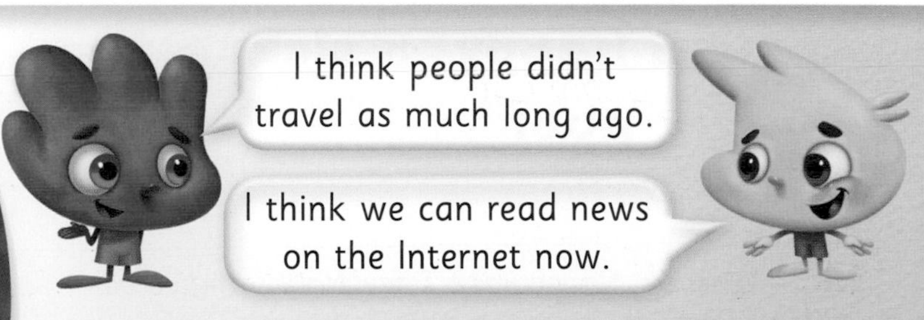

I think people didn't travel as much long ago.
I think we can read news on the Internet now.

Get Ready

Words

A Listen and point to the words. Listen again and say the words. 1•39

arrive

ask

check

enter

poor

crowded

clerk

visit

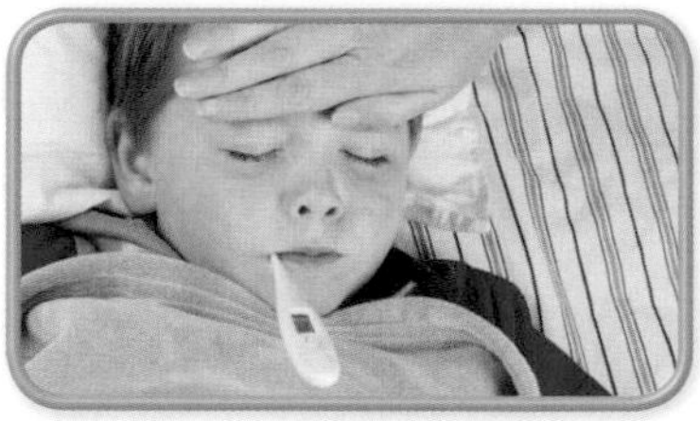

sick

B Complete the sentences. Circle the two correct words.

1 The … checks something.
a doctor b clerk
c balloon

2 He wants to … the zoo.
a visit b jump c go to

3 She's sad because she is …
a happy b sick
c poor

4 The ship is very …
a sugar b crowded
c big

5 I like to … questions.
a ask b walk c answer

6 He arrives at school and … his classroom.
a enters b sees c asks

Before You Read

Think **Are there children from other countries in your school? Do you sometimes visit other towns?**

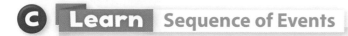

C **Learn** Sequence of Events

Sequence is the order of things, such as 1, 2, 3, 4 or a, b, c, d.

Stories often have a sequence. Events in a story happen in an order:

1 **Grace mailed a letter from Paris to her cousin in London.**
2 **The letter arrived in ten days.**
3 **Her cousin was happy to get the letter.**

Put the events in the correct order. Write the numbers.

☐	Lucia was sad to say goodbye.
☐	She visited her aunt in the city.
1	Lucia lived in a village long ago.
☐	She and her aunt visited many fun places.
☐	She arrived in two days.

D **Long ago, a boy and his family traveled to the United States from far away. How do you think they traveled?**

PREVIEW

Tell Me a Story, Grandpa

This story is *historical fiction*. Historical fiction is a story about something that happened long ago.

Tell Me a Story, Grandpa

"Tell me a story Grandpa!"

"Okay," says Grandpa. "I'll tell you a story about my grandfather, Carlo. In 1910, Carlo was ten years old. He and his family lived in Italy. They were very poor, so they came to the United States for a better life. This was the first time that Carlo traveled to a place far away."

"Really? I'm ten, too," says Henry, "And Mom, Dad, and I visit a different country every summer!"

"Yes, Henry. Things are different now," says Grandpa.

"How did they travel here?" asks Henry.

"They traveled by ship," says Grandpa. "It wasn't an easy trip because the ship was crowded and dirty. There wasn't much food and many people got sick. Carlo was sick too. They arrived at Ellis Island in New York after ten days."

"Wow! That's slow!" says Henry. "Now it only takes about nine hours in an airplane."

"I know," says Grandpa. "It's very different today."

"What happened at Ellis Island?" asks Henry.

"Doctors checked everyone, and Carlo was very scared," says Grandpa.

"Why was he scared, Grandpa? Doctors help people," says Henry.

"Yes. But people who weren't healthy couldn't enter New York," says Grandpa. "The clerks asked them many questions."

"What questions, Grandpa?" asks Henry.

"Where are you from? Are you healthy or are you sick?" says Grandpa. "Luckily, Carlo was feeling better so they let him in. And that's why we live here today and not in Italy."

"That was a cool story, Grandpa!" says Henry. "I have an idea. Let's take a trip to Italy."

"That's a good idea, Henry," says Grandpa. "Let's go next summer."

"Awesome, Grandpa! But let's take an airplane, not a ship!"

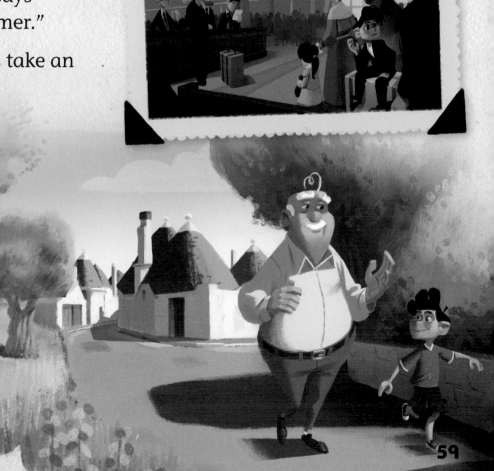

Understand

Comprehension

Think **What do you like about the story? Check (✓). Why? Give one reason.**

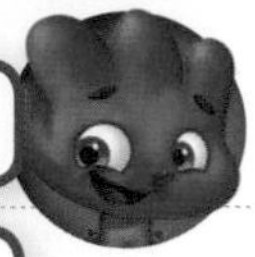 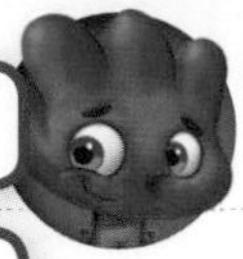 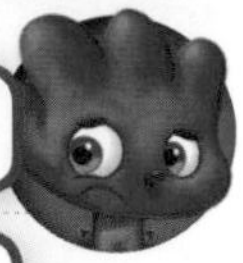

1	The trip to the United States	☐	☐	☐
2	Carlo and his family at Ellis Island	☐	☐	☐
3	Henry's idea of a trip to Italy	☐	☐	☐

A **Ask and answer the question.**

What's your favorite part?

The trip on the ship. It was dangerous.

B **Number the events in the correct order.**

☐ Carlo and his family traveled to the United States on a ship.	☐ Carlo and his family live in the United States.
☐ Carlo and his family arrived at Ellis Island.	☐ The clerks asked Carlo questions.
☐ Carlo and his family entered New York.	1 Carlo and his family lived in Italy.

C **Complete the sentences. Write the words.**

1 Carlo is Grandpa's ______________.

2 Henry is ______________ years old.

3 Ellis island is in ______________.

4 Henry wants to go to Italy by ______________.

Think **What do you think?**

1 Is Henry happy that he lives now and not long ago? Why?

2 Was it easy going to a new country long ago?

Grammar in Use

D Listen and sing along. **What Did You Do Yesterday?** 1•41

What did you do yesterday?
Did you visit May? Yes, I did.
Did you walk there in the rain?
Did you travel there by train?
What did you do yesterday?

What did you do yesterday?
Did you travel far? No, I didn't.
Did you climb up a tree?
Did you watch shows on TV?
What did you do yesterday?

E **Learn Grammar** Simple Past Regular Verbs

Did they travel by ship? Yes, they did.

Did they arrive in two days? No, they didn't.

What did they do? They liv<u>ed</u> with Carlo's uncle.

Where did they go? How did they travel there? Practice with a partner.

Grandpa Joe
Grandma Mae
Grandpa Leo
Grandma Helen
Where did he travel?
He traveled to New York.
Did he travel by ship?
Yes, he did.
Is it ... ?

F **Ask your partner a question about how he or she traveled to school today.**

Communicate

Words

A Listen and point to the words. Listen again and say the words. 1•42

couch

chair

lamp

clock

bathtub

sink

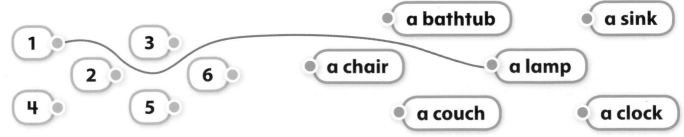

B Read the sentences. Write the words from **A**. You can use the same word more than once.

1	What are three things we can sit in or on?	couch ______ ______
2	What are two things we wash in?	______ ______
3	What are three things we can see in a bedroom?	______ ______ ______
4	What are two things we can see in a classroom?	______ ______

Listening

Think What are some old things in your home?

C Listen. Why were some things small a long time ago? 1•43

D Listen again and match. 1•44

1 2 3 4 5 6

a bathtub a sink a chair a lamp a couch a clock

Speaking

E **Imagine you traveled between two cities in your country a long time ago. Practice with your partner. Use the words in the boxes to help.** 1•45

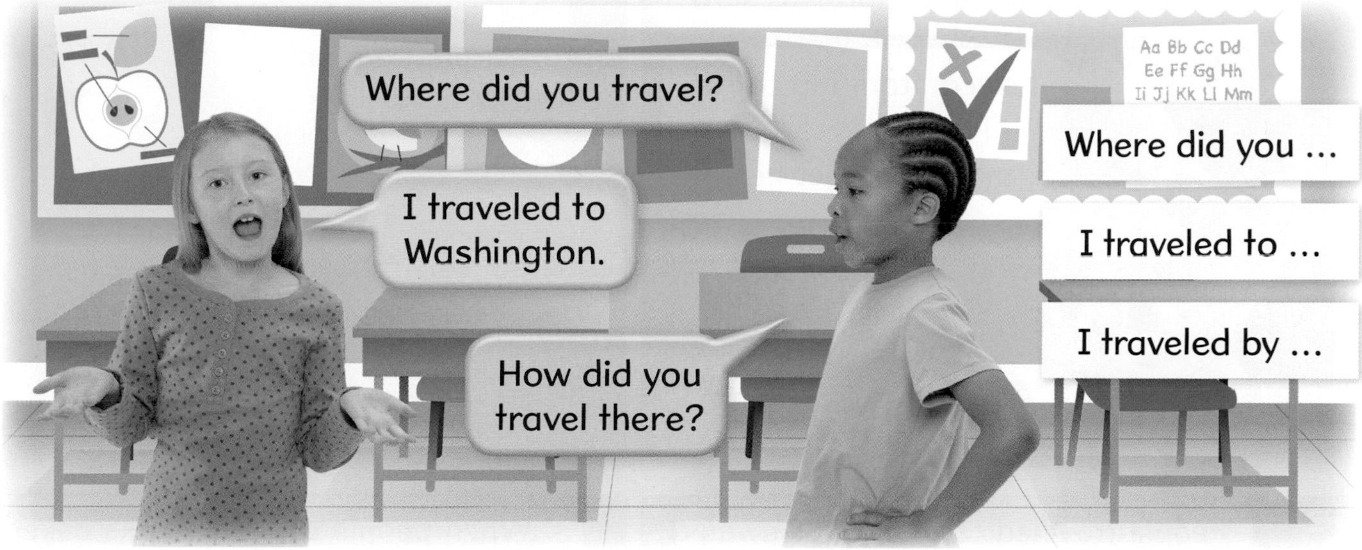

Aa Bb Cc Dd
Ee Ff Gg Hh
Ii Jj Kk Ll Mm
Where did you travel?
I traveled to Washington.
How did you travel there?
Where did you ...
I traveled to ...
I traveled by ...

Writing Study

F **Learn** Adding *-ed* to Some Verbs

When we talk about things in the past, we add -ed to some verbs.

I visited my grandmother.

If the verb ends in e, we just add d.

He arrived in New York yesterday.

Complete the sentences. Write the past tense verbs.

1 My grandfather traveled to New York in 1910. (travel)

2 Lisa ______________ late for school. (arrive)

3 My brother ______________ ball in the park. (play)

4 We ______________ the building together. (enter)

Write **Tell your partner about traveling to a place 100 years ago and traveling there today. Write about it in your Workbook.** page 53

Wrap Up

A Listen and read along. 1•46

This is our play about life long ago. Communication was slow.
Letters from my cousin in New York take two months to get here!
My cousin is coming from London!
Arrgghh!
People traveled to places far away by ship. It was slow and difficult.
It's crowded and dirty.
When people arrived, clerks asked questions and doctors checked people.
Do you have family here?
Yes, a cousin.
People used a horse and cart to travel to places nearby.
Hello, cousin from London!
Hello! I'm so tired!
Today it's easy and fast to communicate and travel. We have...
Internet, e-mail ...
... and airplanes! Phew!

Project: Interview an Adult

B Interview an adult.

- Ask him or her questions about life now and long ago.
- Write a report of the interview.
- Draw or find pictures.

C Put your interview on the wall. Tell the class one interesting thing from the interview.

My grandmother listened to the radio a long time ago. She watches TV every night now.

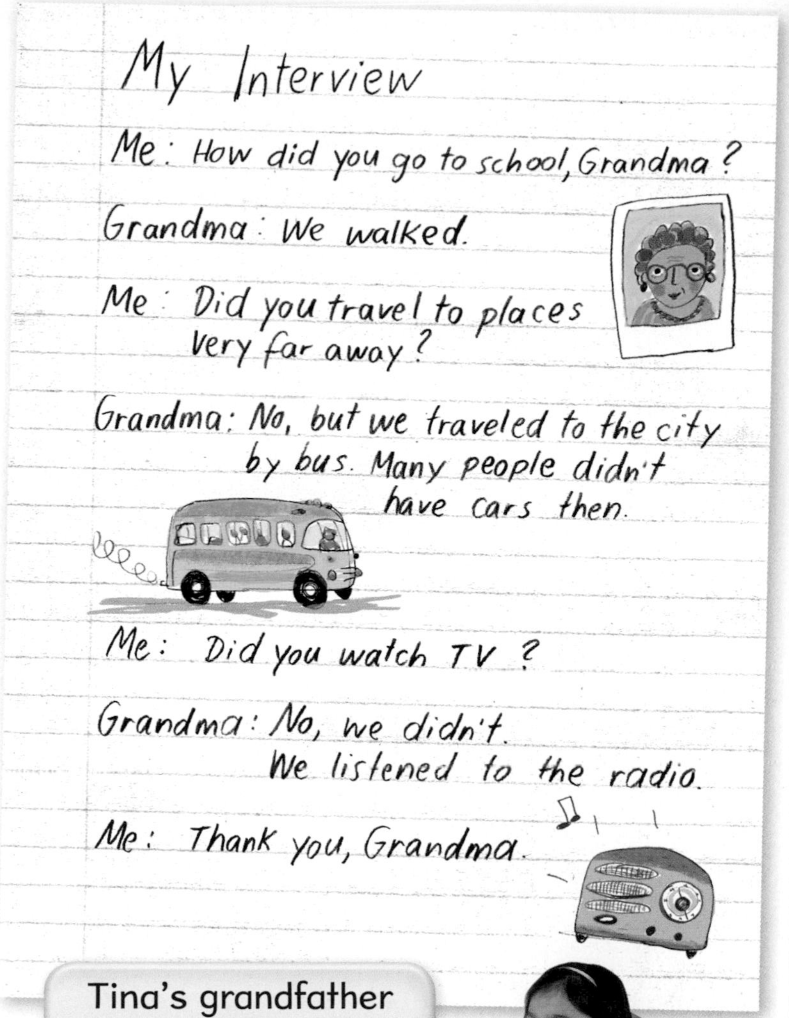

My Interview

Me: How did you go to school, Grandma?

Grandma: We walked.

Me: Did you travel to places very far away?

Grandma: No, but we traveled to the city by bus. Many people didn't have cars then.

Me: Did you watch TV?

Grandma: No, we didn't. We listened to the radio.

Me: Thank you, Grandma.

D Walk around the room. Look at all the interviews. Say one thing about each interview.

Tina's grandfather lived in New York a long time ago. He lives in Boston now.

BIG QUESTION 3

How are things different now from long ago?

A Watch the video.

B Think more about the Big Question.

C Complete the **Big Question Chart.**

What did you learn about how things are different from long ago?

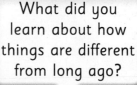

In units **7** and **8** you will:

WATCH a video about subtraction.

LEARN about subtraction.

READ about a greedy monkey.

WRITE a subtraction word problem.

MAKE and play a board game.

BIG QUESTION 4

When do we use subtraction?

A **Watch the video.** ▶

B **Look at the picture. What do you see?**

1 What does the boy have?

2 What is he doing?

C **Think and answer the questions.**

1 When do we use numbers?

2 How much money did you have two days ago? How much do you have now?

D **Fill out the Big Question Chart.**

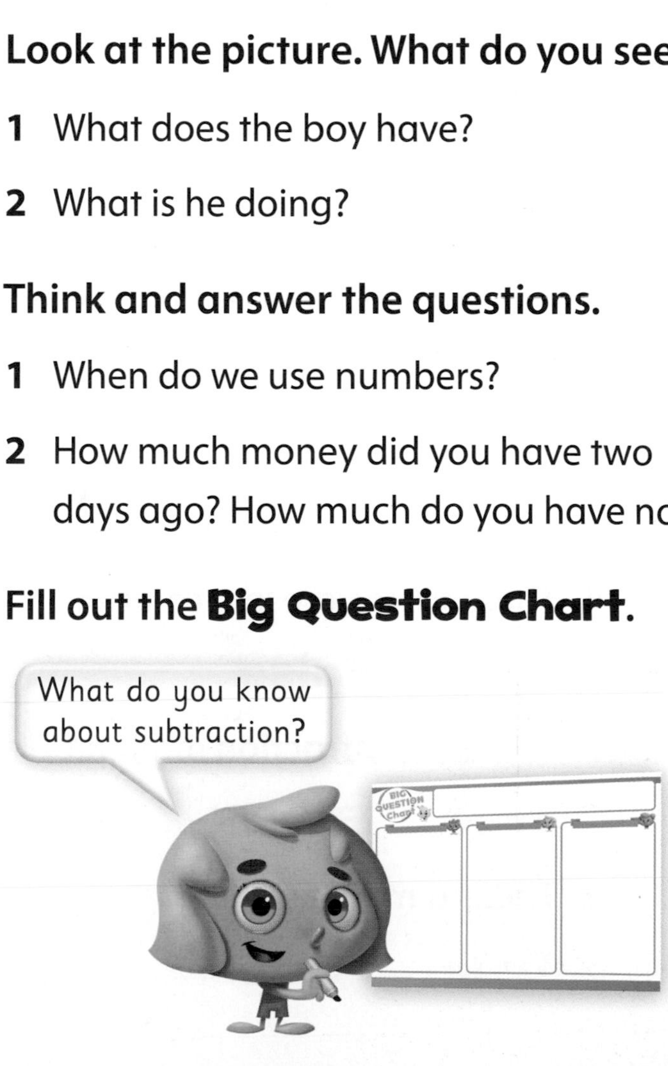
What do you know about subtraction?

UNIT 7 Get Ready

Words

A **Listen and point to the words. Listen again and say the words.** 1•47

minus sign

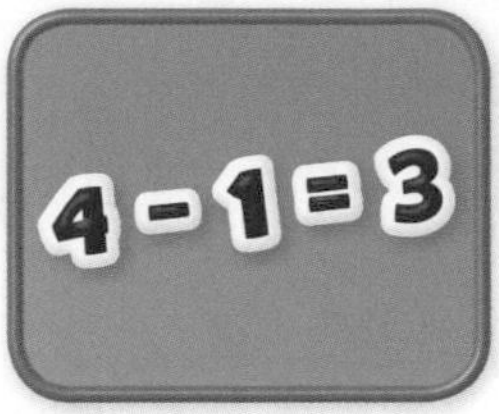

subtraction

take away

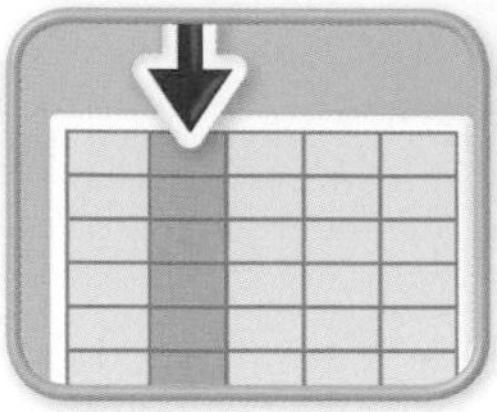

column

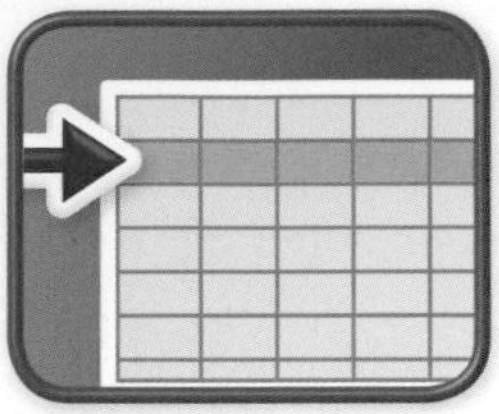

row

test score

single-digit number

double-digit number

left

B **Circle the correct answer.**

1 There are 43 apples. I **take away** 5 apples. There are 2 apples **left**.

True (False)

2 These are **single-digit numbers:** 1, 4, and 9.

True False

3 When your **test score** is bad, your teacher isn't happy.

True False

4 These things are in a **column**.

True False

5 This is a **subtraction** math problem.

True False

6 This is a **minus sign**.

True False

Before You Read

Think Do you like math? What's your favorite number?

C **Learn** Reread

To **reread** means to read a text again. You can reread something for many different reasons, such as when you don't understand something. When you reread, read slowly and think about what you're reading.

Read the text once. Answer the questions.

We use math every day. People use addition and subtraction when they buy and sell things. Your parents use math when they buy food and clothes for you, so they know how much money they need. You use math to keep score when you play a game with your friends.

1 When do people use subtraction? ____________

2 When do you use math? ____________

Now reread the text. Answer the question.

1 Why do parents use math? ____________

____

D **The text on pages 70 –71 is about subtraction. What are the three words you think are in the text?**

PREVIEW

Subtraction

In this text, we learn about subtraction.

This text is an *informational text*. Remember, informational texts tell us about our world.

Math

Read 1·48

Subtraction

What is subtraction?

When we add things, we join them together. When we subtract things, we take them away from other things. Then we can see how many things are left.

There are 3 apples left.

Subtracting in Groups

When we count backward, we're subtracting 1 each time. Count backward from 50 to 1. Now count backward by fives, subtracting 5 each time. Now count backward by tens. How much are you subtracting each time now?

Think
Reread this part.

50 | 45 | 40 | 35 | 30 | 25 | 20 | 15 | 10 | 5 | 0

Subtraction Math Problems

All subtraction math problems have a minus sign.

This is the minus sign. The minus sign tells us to subtract 4 from 9.

This is the answer. It tells how many are left.

We write $9 - 4 = 5$.

$$9 - 4 = 5$$

We say "Nine minus four equals five."

Subtraction Math Problems in Rows and Columns

$$5 - 2 = 3$$

We usually write subtraction math problems for single-digit numbers in a row and we usually write subtraction problems for double-digit numbers in a column.

$$\begin{array}{r} 50 \\ -\ 20 \\ \hline 30 \end{array}$$

Think

Reread this part.

Subtraction Word Problems

Let's use subtraction to solve these problems.

Alma bought five cookies. Her friends ate three. How many cookies were left?

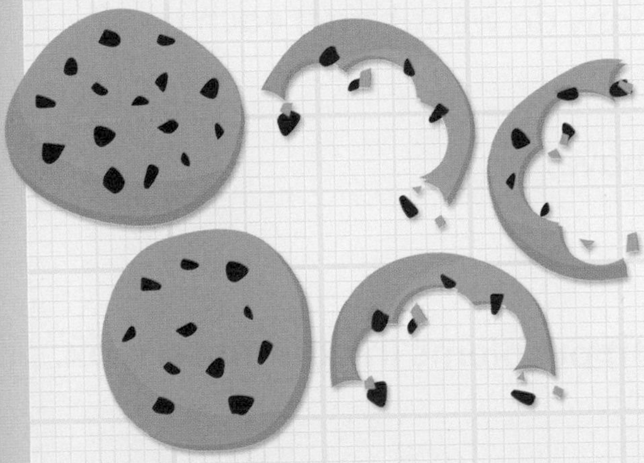

$$5 - 3 = ?$$

Olivia had thirty-five grapes. She gave twenty grapes to her little sister. How many grapes were left?

$$\begin{array}{r} 35 \\ -\ 20 \\ \hline = \ ? \end{array}$$

Now think of some things that people subtract every day.

My teacher subtracts numbers from 100 for my test score!

Understand

Comprehension

Think **What do you like about the text? Check (✓). Why? Give one reason.**

 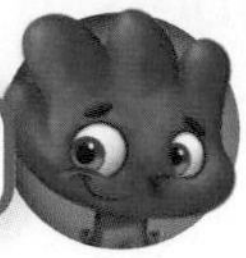 

1 Counting backwards in fives and tens	☐	☐	☐
2 Subtraction math problems in rows and columns	☐	☐	☐
3 Subtraction word problems	☐	☐	☐

A **Ask and answer the question.**

What's your favorite part?
Counting backwards in tens. It's fast.

B **Answer the questions.**

1 When we count backward in twenties, how many do we subtract each time?

____

2 What sign do all subtraction math problems have?

____

C **Use these numbers to write subtraction math problems in your notebook. Use rows and columns.**

1 (50) (15) (35) 2 (75) (50) (25) 3 (8) (4) (4)

Think **What do you think?**

1 When do we count backwards?
2 Why can we write single-digit subtraction problems in rows?

Workbook Grammar
pages 060–061

Grammar in Use

D **Listen and sing along.** **Cookies!** 1-49

Yesterday, Billy bought cookies at the store.
He bought sixteen cookies, but his sister ate four.
His mother ate three, and his brother had eight.
How many cookies were left on Billy's plate?

Today, Billy didn't buy cookies at the store.
But his mother bought three and his sister bought four.
His brother bought sixteen but he only had eight.
How many cookies were left on Billy's plate?

E **Learn Grammar** **Simple Past Irregular Verbs**

Alma bought five cookies. She didn't buy four.
Olivia gave her sister twenty stickers.
She didn't give her twenty-six.

eat > ate	see > saw	buy > bought

What did they do? Practice with a partner.

May	eat		✓		✗
Tam	see		✓		✗
Jay	buy		✓		✗

F **Tell your partner something you did and didn't eat or drink yesterday.**

Communicate

Words

A **Listen and point to the words. Listen again and say the words.** 1•50

clean	**dirty**	**tired**	**hungry**	**thirsty**	**full**

B **Match the words to the sentences.**

1 clean	**a** I ate ten cookies!
2 dirty	**b** I want some water, please.
3 tired	**c** I want chicken and rice, please.
4 hungry	**d** I have a new, white dress.
5 thirsty	**e** I want to sleep.
6 full	**f** I am washing my clothes.

Listening

Think **How do you feel now?**

C **Listen. What do the kittens drink?** 1•51

D **Listen again and circle the correct subtraction problem. Then write the answer.** 1•52

1	60 - 30	60 - 13	**3**	40 - 13	14 - 13	**5**	16 - 15	60 - 50
2	19 - 17	90 - 17	**4**	18 - 15	80 - 50	**6**	17 - 11	70 - 11

Speaking

E Listen and repeat. Then practice with a partner. Use the words in the box to help. 1•53

pasta salad soup
I'm not hungry.
I don't like it.
I just ate some.
tea juice soda

Word Study

F **Learn** Syllables

A word can have more than one part. These parts are called **syllables**. Each syllable is a separate sound.

One-syllable words: **ate, test, salt**
Two-syllable words: **dou / ble, bath / tub**
Three-syllable words: **an / i / mal, sub / trac / tion**

Mark the syllables. Write the number.

1 fea / ther ___2___
2 ice ______
3 instrument ______
4 message ______
5 liquid ______
6 vacation ______

Write Think of an interesting subtraction problem with your partner. Now write about it in your **Workbook**. page 63

BIG QUESTION 4

When do we use subtraction?

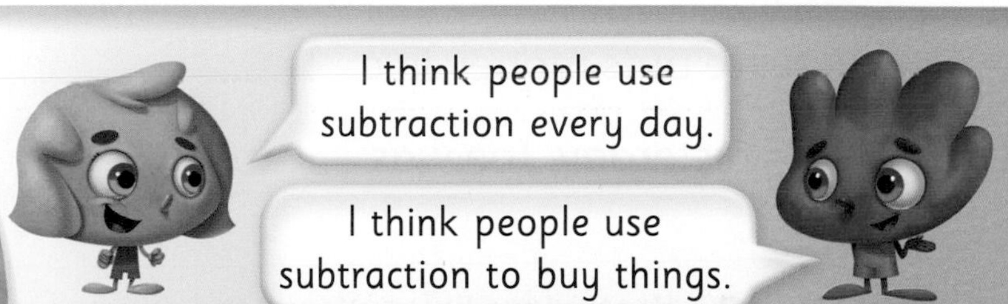

I think people use subtraction every day.
I think people use subtraction to buy things.

UNIT 8 Get Ready

Words

A Listen and point to the words. Listen again and say the words. 2•02

let go

steal

dig up

hide

jar

greedy

bored

baker

cook

B Look at **A** and write the words.

1 People who work in a kitchen: baker ______________

2 Things we can do: ______________ ______________ ______________ ______________

C Complete the sentences. Write the words from **A**.

1 When it rains, I feel ______________ and don't know what to do.

2 He puts money in a ______________ every day so he can buy a bike.

3 Yesterday, Joe was ______________ and ate too many cakes.

Before You Read

Think What kind of candy do you like? What animals can dig things up?

D **Learn** Beginning, Middle, and End of a Story

Stories have three parts.

- **a beginning**: Mary baked ten cookies for her friends.
- **a middle**: Her brothers were hungry and ate eight cookies.
- **an end**: Mary only had two cookies left for her friends.

Read the sentences. Number them in the correct order. Then write B (beginning) for two sentences, M (middle) for three sentences, and E (end) for two sentences.

☐ His test grade is good. ______

☐ She takes away ten points. ______

☐ He takes the test and writes the answers. ______

1 Aaron has a subtraction test today. __B__

☐ He likes math now. ______

☐ Ms. Jackson grades Aaron's test. ______

☐ His score is 90. ______

E **Look at the pictures on pages 78–79. What places do you think are in the story?**

PREVIEW

Bandar, the Greedy Monkey

This story is a *fable*. A fable is a story that teaches us a lesson. Bandar means monkey, in Hindi. Some people in India speak Hindi.

Read 2•03

Bandar, the Greedy Monkey

A monkey called Bandar lived in the woods near a small town. One day, Bandar was bored and decided to go into the town.

Bandar went to a bakery and saw thirty beautiful cookies. He stole a cookie and ate it. It was good! He ate more and more cookies!

The baker saw Bandar and chased him. "You greedy little monkey!" he cried. "Now there are only fifteen cookies!"

Bandar ran up a tree and hid in the leaves. When he looked down, he saw sixty small carrots in a garden. When the gardener wasn't looking, Bandar ran down the tree, dug up a carrot, and ate it. It was good! He ate more and more carrots!

The gardener saw Bandar and chased him. "You greedy little monkey! Now there are only forty-four carrots!"

Bandar went to a restaurant and saw forty-two sausages. He stole a sausage and ate it. It was good! He ate more and more sausages!

The cook saw Bandar and chased him.
"You greedy little monkey! Now there are only thirty sausages!"

Bandar stole food all over the town. Everyone was angry. They tried to catch Bandar, but he was too fast. Then the candy maker had an idea.

The next day, Bandar went to the candy store. He saw two big jars of candy in every color, and it all looked good! Bandar put his hands in the jars and grabbed twenty pieces of candy. But he couldn't get the candy out of the jars.

The candy maker ran in.
"You greedy little monkey! Let go of the candy and you can run away!"

Did Bandar let go of the candy?
No, he didn't, and the candy maker caught him. He took him back to the woods and told him never to come to town again.

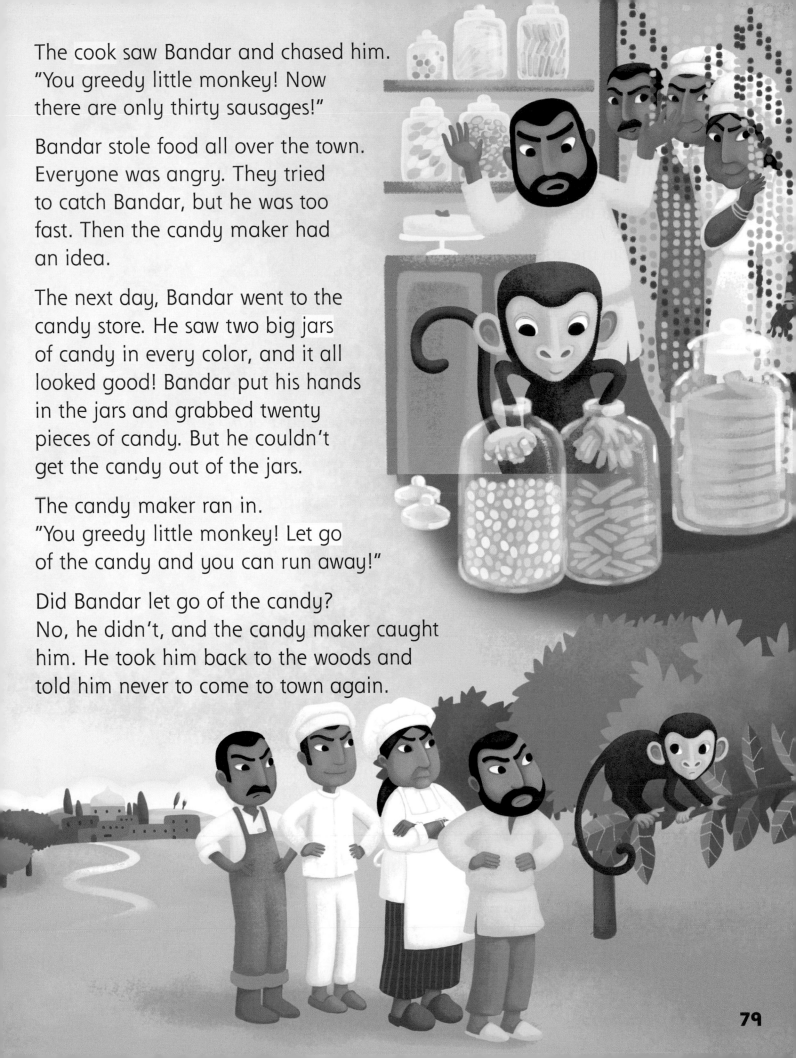

Understand

Comprehension

Think **What do you like about the story? Check (✓). Why? Give one reason.**

1 Bandar at the bakery ☐ ☐ ☐
2 Bandar in the garden ☐ ☐ ☐
3 Bandar in the candy store ☐ ☐ ☐

A Ask and answer the question.

What's your favorite part?

Greedy Bandar didn't let go of the candy. It's funny.

B Look at the pictures. Number them in the correct order. Then write B (beginning), M (middle), and E (end).

☐ 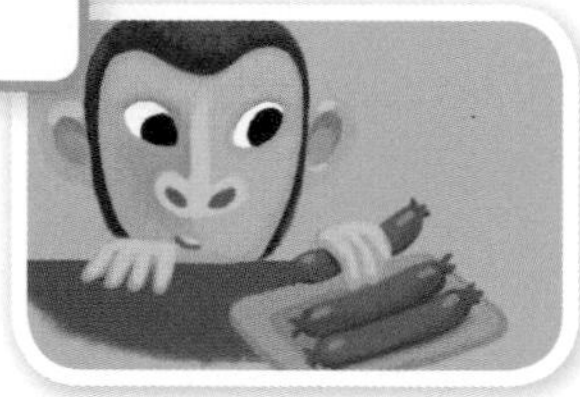 ______

☐  ______

☐  ______

C Read the subtraction word problems. Answer the questions.

1 The baker had thirty cookies. Now he has fifteen.
How many cookies did Bandar steal? ______ cookies

2 The gardener had sixty carrots. Now he has forty-four.
How many carrots did Bandar dig up? ______ carrots

Think **What do you think?**

1 Was Bandar a smart monkey?
2 What is the lesson of the story? Give one idea.

Grammar in Use

D **Listen and sing along.** **Where Are My Toys?** 2·04

Where's my kite, and where's my ball?
Did I leave them in the hall?
What did I do with my toy train?
Did I leave it out again?

Where's my robot? Where's my car?
I don't know where my toys are.
Did I have them yesterday?
Did I put them all away?

Here's my kite, and here's my ball!
I didn't loose them after all!
Mom put all my toys away!
Here they are! It's time to play!

E **Learn Grammar** **Simple Past Irregular Verbs**

Did Bandar go to a candy store? Yes, he did.
Did he let go of the candy? No, he didn't.
What did Bandar do with the cookies? He ate them.

Follow the lines. Ask your partner the questions.

make > made buy > bought take > took sell > sold

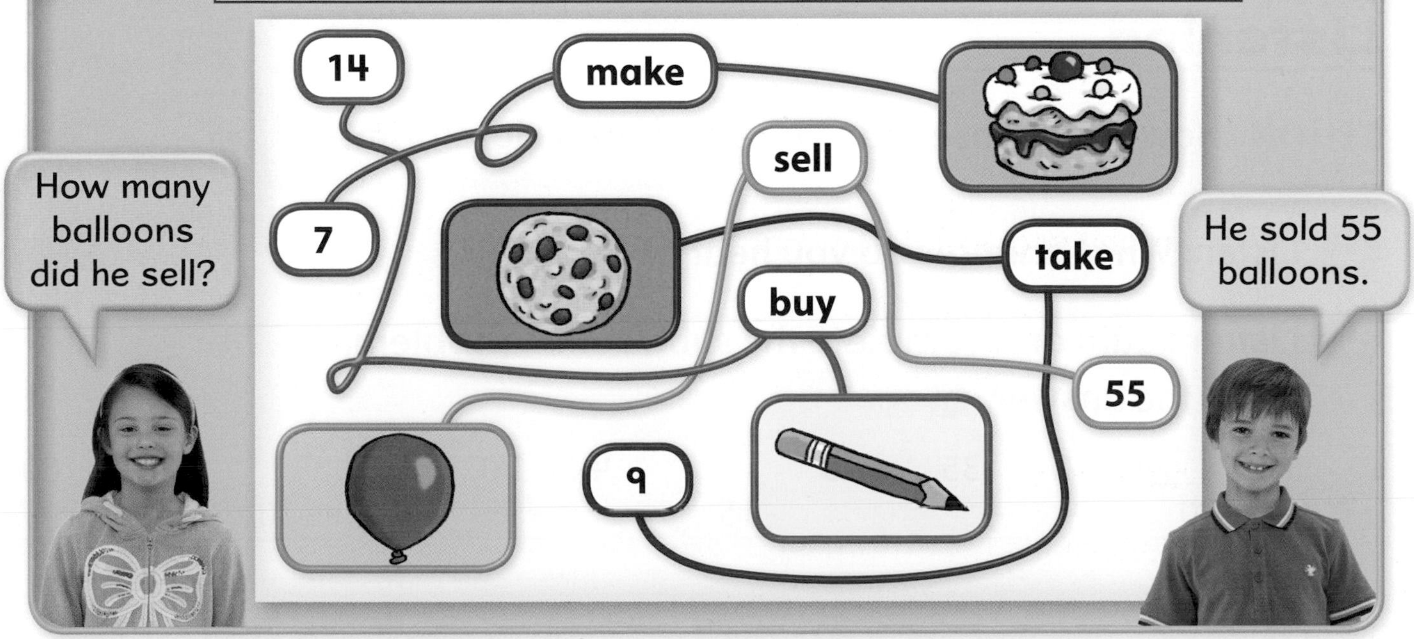

Communicate

Words

A **Listen and point to the words. Listen again and say the words.** 2•05

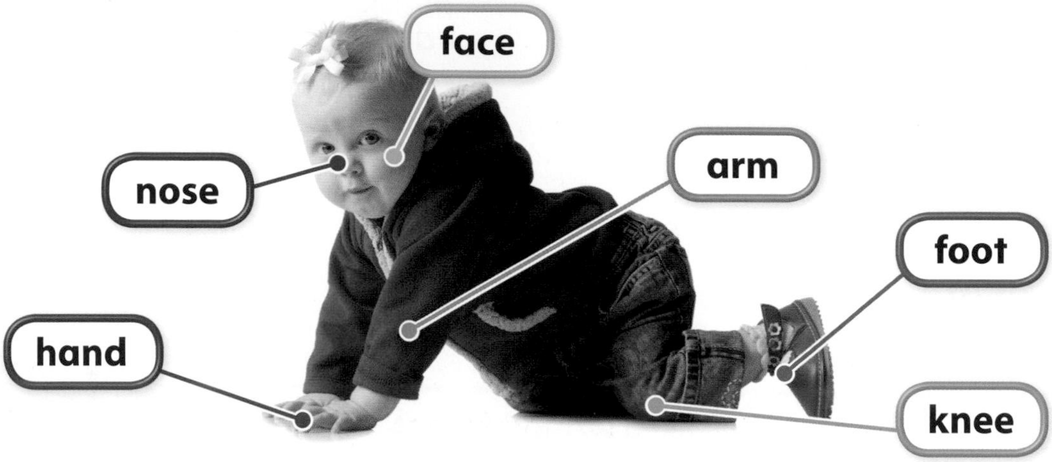

B **Read the sentences. Write the words from A.**

1 Most animals don't have these but orangutans have very long ones. arms

2 People and animals use it to smell. ________

3 People use these to clap. We should keep them clean to stay healthy. ________

4 Your eyes, nose, and mouth are on this body part. ________

5 We put sneakers on these. ________

6 This is in the middle of your leg. ________

Listening

Think **How many noses can you see in your classroom?**

C **Listen. What animals do you hear about?** 2•06

D **Listen again and complete the subtraction problem. Write the answer.** 2•07

1	2	3	4	5	6
____	35	____	70	____	60
- 20	- ____	- 15	- ____	- 10	- ____
____	____	____	____	____	____

Speaking

E **Make a crazy subtraction problem poem by replacing the colored words with your own. Tell your partner. Use the words in the boxes to help.** 2•08

Twenty cows sat in some trees.
Five fell down and hurt their knees.
How many cows were left in the trees?
Aa Bb Cc Dd
Ee Ff Gg Hh
Ii Jj Kk Ll Mm
Thirty eagles ...
Seven ...
How many ...
Fifteen cows were left in the trees.

Writing Study

F **Learn** Contractions

Remember, contractions are two words joined together. We make contractions by taking away a letter and adding an apostrophe (').

do + not = don't **does + not** = doesn't **did + not** = didn't
can + not = can't **should + not** = shouldn't

Write the contractions.

1 Karen doesn't like fruit salad. (does not)

2 Bandar ______ dig up carrots in the garden. (should not)

3 Kamil ______ play a musical instrument. (can not)

4 Bandar ______ let go of the candy. (did not)

5 Mammals ______ have wings or gills. (do not)

Write **Tell your partner three things you did last night.**
Now write about them in your Workbook. page 71

Wrap Up

A Listen and read along. 2•09

The students' subtraction test scores were very good!

The class played a game. Two students let go. How many students were left?

The class sang and danced. Three students hid in the bushes. How many were left?

They had thirteen sandwiches. The birds stole eight. How many were left?

There were twenty-four cookies. Gus ate ten. How many cookies were left?

Ms. Smart took a picture of the class. They were tired, hungry, and thirsty, but they were happy.

Project: Make a Subtraction Board Game

B **Make a subtraction board game.**

- Draw the squares.
- Think of the subtraction problems.
- Write the problems in the squares.

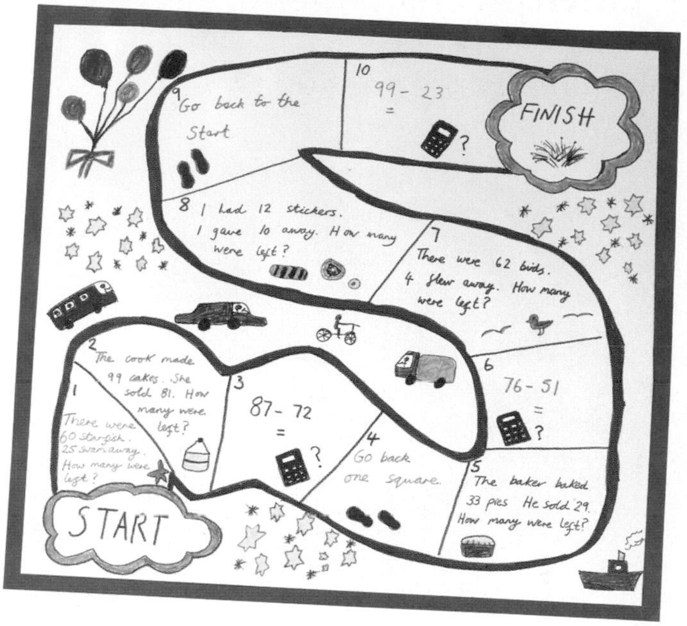

C **Switch games with another group. Play the board game. Write down your answers.**

The baker baked 33 pies.
He sold 29.
How many pies were left?
Four pies were left!

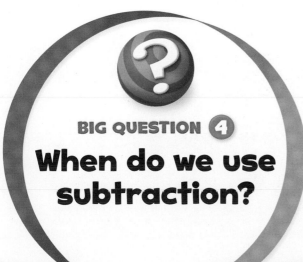

D **Give your board game back to the group to check the answers.**

BIG QUESTION 4

When do we use subtraction?

A **Watch the video.** ▶

B **Think more about the Big Question.**

C Complete the **Big Question Chart.**

What did you learn about subtraction?

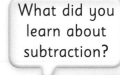

In units **9** and **10** you will:

WATCH
a video about people getting along.

LEARN
about rules.

READ
poems about how to get along with people.

WRITE about rules at home.

MAKE a rules poster.

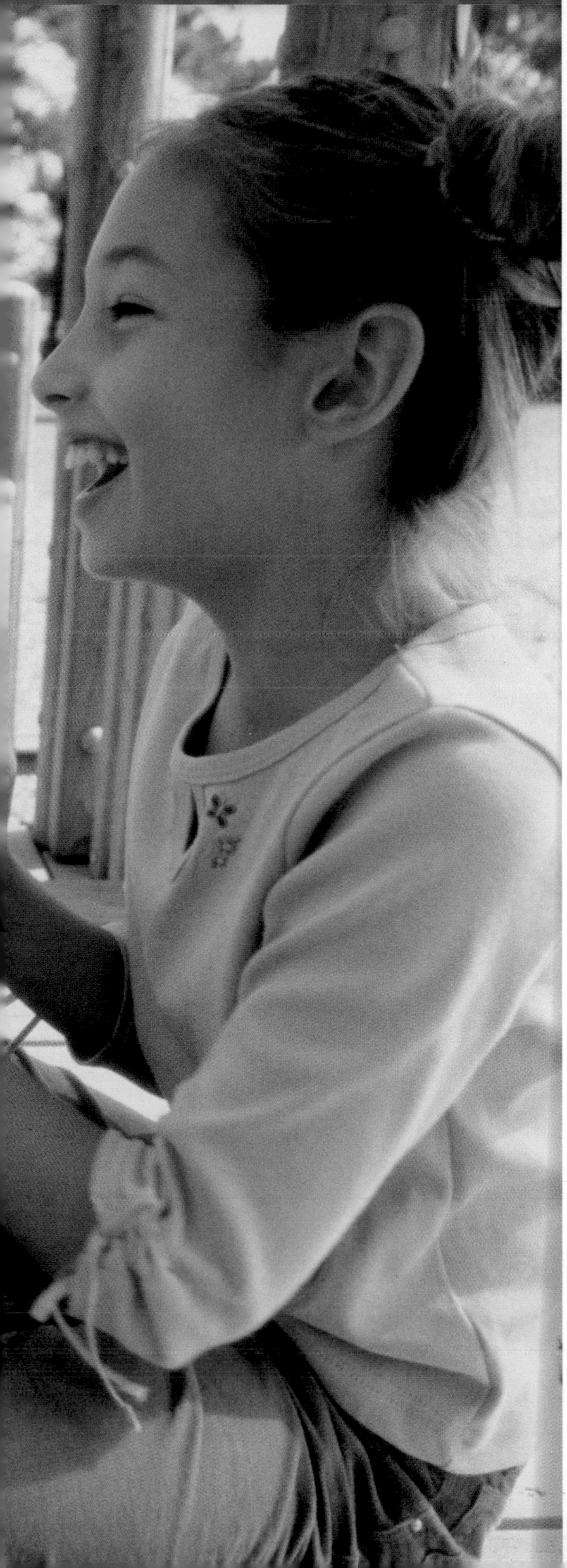

BIG QUESTION 5

How do people get along with each other?

A Watch the video.

B Look at the picture. What do you see?

1 What are the girls doing?

2 Where are they?

C Think and answer the questions.

1 How can you help your teacher?

2 What do your parents do for you?

D Fill out the **Big Question Chart**.

What do you know about how people get along with each other?

Get Ready

Words

A Listen and point to the words. Listen again and say the words. 2•10

traffic light

take turns

polite

clean up

litter

librarian

crossing guard

principal

lifeguard

B One of the words is incorrect. Cross out the wrong answer.

1 She works in a school. She helps the students find books.
a **librarian** b ~~**principal**~~

2 We see these on streets. They're red, yellow, and green.
a **litter** b **traffic lights**

3 The bus is full. A boy stands up so an old woman can sit down.
a **polite** b **patient**

4 The library is messy. The student puts the books away.
a **clean up** b **take turns**

5 He works at a swimming pool.
a **crossing guard** b **lifeguard**

Before You Read

Think **What things can you do at home? What things can't you do at school?**

C **Learn** Categorize

When we categorize, we put things that are similar into groups. After you read, think of the things you read about. How are they similar? Can they be put in one group? This helps you to remember them later.

Pasta, vegetables, and salad are in the food group.

Jackets, shorts, and T-shirts are in the clothes group.

Read the text. Complete the chart.

A reserve worker talks to some children. "Those are orangutans. They're mammals, and their bodies are covered in hair. They have two arms and two legs."

"Those orange-and-red tree frogs are amphibians and live in trees. They have wet skin on their bodies. They have long legs so they can jump high."

Animals	Body Coverings	Body Parts
1 mammals		
2 amphibians		

D **Look at the title and pictures on pages 90–91. What do you think the text is about?**

PREVIEW

Following Rules

This text is an *informational text*. Remember, informational texts tell us about our world.

Social Studies: Community

Read 2•11

Following Rules

We follow rules every day. There are rules for things we do at home, at school, and in a lot of other places.

Think about rules at home. Parents usually make these rules, and they make sure we follow them. Parents can ask us to wash our hands and clean up. They make other rules about eating unhealthy food, watching TV, or bedtime. What rules do you follow at home?

There are rules at school, too. Teachers and the principal make the school rules. We should always be polite and take turns when we play games. Librarians help us follow the rules in the school library. We can't eat, drink, or be noisy there. Outside school, the crossing guard helps us cross the road safely, and we should pay attention to the traffic light. These rules help keep us happy and safe. Can you think of more rules at school?

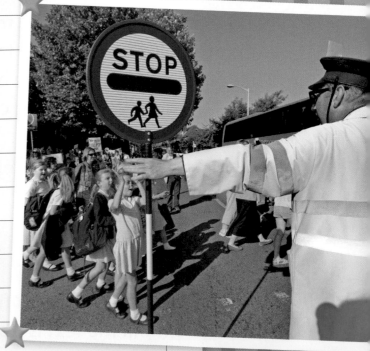

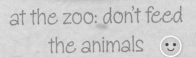

at the zoo: don't feed the animals

Zoos and other fun places have rules, too. At the zoo, you can't touch or feed the animals. You should never throw things at the animals.

Think

How do these rules help the animals?

Swimming pools are fun places, too. These rules help make it safe for everyone there. You shouldn't run near the water and you can't eat, drink, or litter near the pool. You must always listen to the lifeguards because lifeguards make sure we follow the rules and that we are safe in and near the water.

Think

How can these rules help us have fun?

Rules tell us what we should and shouldn't do, and they help keep us safe, happy, and healthy. What rules do you think are important?

Understand

Comprehension

Think **What do you like about the text? Check (✓). Why? Give one reason.**

1 Rules at home	☐	☐	☐
2 Rules at school	☐	☐	☐
3 Rules at fun places	☐	☐	☐

A **Ask and answer the question.**

What's your favorite part?

Rules at the zoo help to keep animals safe. That's good!

B **Complete the chart. Write the words from the text.**

These people help keep us safe.	These places have rules.
1 parents	1
2	2
3	3
4	4
5	5

C **Answer the questions.**

1 Who make rules at school? ________________

2 What should we do when we play games? ________________

Think **What do you think?**

1 Are rules only for children?

2 Can we follow rules and have fun, too?

Grammar in Use

D **Listen and sing along.** **Whose Shoes Are These?** 2•12

Oh dear, whose shoes are these?
Help me clean up, please.
These are mine and those are yours.
Are these Layla's? Yes, of course.
They are Layla's shoes.

No, no, that isn't right,
No, no hers are white.
These are mine and those are yours.
Are these Layla's? Yes, of course.
They are Layla's shoes.

E **Learn Grammar** **Possessive Pronouns**

Those are your things. Those things are **yours**.

They aren't my toys. They aren't **mine**.

Whose book is this? It's **hers**.

Whose pencils are these? They're **his**.

Ask questions about what people in your group have.

Whose pencils are these?
They're his.

Whose notebook is this?
It's mine!

F **Walk around the room with your partner. Point to three things in the classroom and ask questions about who they belong to.**

Words

A Listen and point to the words. Listen again and say the words. 2•13

kitchen

living room

cafeteria

classroom

swimming pool

crosswalk

B Think about the words in **A** and add them to the chart.

Only at School	Only at Home	Both
1 cafeteria	1	1
2		2
3		

Listening

Think Is there a crossing guard at the crosswalk at your school?

C Listen. Where is it dangerous to run around? 2•14

D Listen again and circle the correct places. 2•15

These are rules for the ...	
1 cafeteria	crosswalk
2 living room	kitchen
3 zoo	swimming pool
4 library	cafeteria
5 kitchen	living room
6 classroom	library

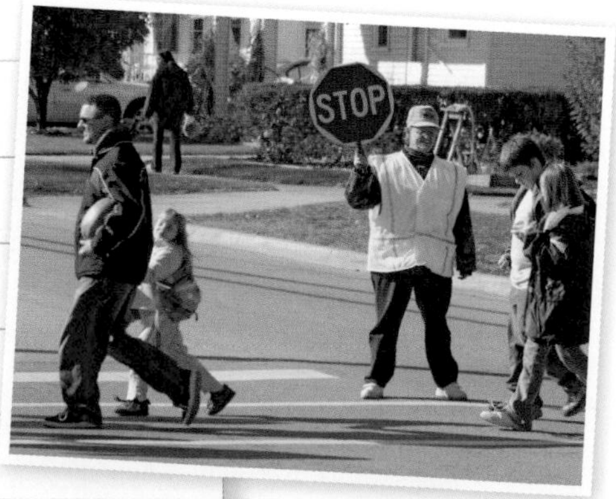

Speaking

E **Listen and repeat. Then practice with a partner. Use the words in the box to help.** 2•16

her our
Sorry about that.
My mistake.
That's all right.
Don't worry about it.

Word Study

F **Learn** Phrasal Verbs

Sometimes two words go together to make one verb that has a special meaning.

Clean up: **Jenny** cleaned up **the kitchen for her mother.**

Write the correct word.

1 Leo and Nancy put ___away___ the pencils and erasers.

2 The rabbit dug ______________ all the carrots.

3 My sister fell ______________ and hurt her arm.

4 The cat ran ______________ from the fox.

away
up
down

Write **Tell your partner about three rules at your house. Does he or she have the same rules? Now write about them in your Workbook.** page 81

BIG QUESTION 5

How do people get along with each other?

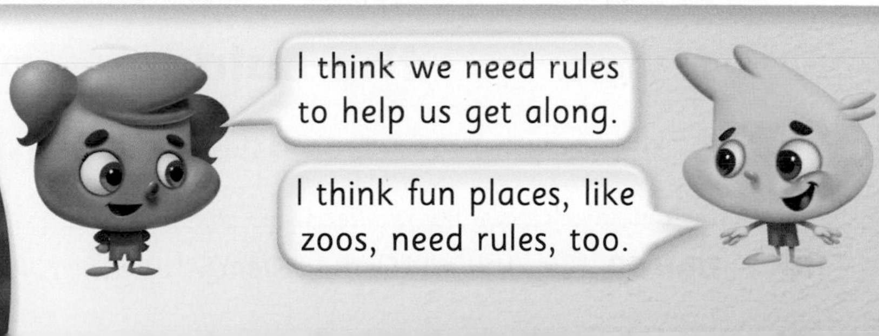

I think we need rules to help us get along.
I think fun places, like zoos, need rules, too.

Get Ready

Words

A Listen and point to the words. Listen again and say the words. 2•17

knock

thoughtful

rude

grab

pass

put away

invite

wash

share

B Circle the one that does not belong.

1 wash:	my hands	a car	gills
2 grab:	steam	a hand	an apple
3 put away:	the books	the bus	the toys
4 knock on:	a cook	the window	the door
5 invite:	my aunt	my friend	traffic lights
6 pass:	the tea	the freezer	the salt
7 share:	the salad	popcorn	the candle
8 be:	scales	thoughtful	rude

Before You Read

Think How are you a good friend? How can you be nice to people?

C **Learn** Theme

The theme of a story is the most important thing the writer wants you to understand. The writer is often showing something important.

Matthew and Dylan are different. Matthew likes math, art, and quiet places, but Dylan doesn't like them. Matthew can sing and dance but Dylan can't. They like each other and e-mail each other every day.

Theme: People who are very different can be friends.

Read the story. Circle the correct theme.

Mouse, Rabbit, and Opossum are hungry. They want dinner but their food is boring because they eat the same food every day. Mouse eats fruit, Opossum eats vegetables, and Rabbit eats carrots. They have an idea. They take their food to Mouse's house. They now have three different foods for dinner. They're happy!

1 It's good to share things.

2 We should eat the same food every day.

D **Look at the pictures on pages 98–99. What animal is rude?**

PREVIEW

THE PLEASE AND THANK YOU BOOK OF POEMS

These texts are *poems*. Poems use words to create a rhythm, or pattern, of beats. The words create pictures in our minds.

Barbara Shook Hazen is the author of over 70 books that children all around the world like to read! She enjoys traveling and writing about animals.

Read 2•18

THE PLEASE AND THANK YOU BOOK OF POEMS

Welcome, Ricky Raccoon

When Ricky Raccoon comes over to play,
He helps put all of the toys away.
He asks his friend what he'd like to do
And is always careful with scissors and glue.

He washes before he comes to the table
And helps his host whenever he's able.
That's why almost every day
Someone invites Ricky over to play.

Think
What is the theme of this poem?

Don't be Grabby, Gorilla

Gorillas are rude.
They grab their food.
They never say,
"Please pass the peach."
They're so anxious,
They just reach.
They upset others
By all they do.
And sometimes ... they upset
The table, too.

Think
What is the theme of this poem?

The Ox Always Knocks

The ox
Always knocks
Before
Opening a door.

Because
Someone behind it
Might be sleeping.
Or wrapping a present,
Or sad or weeping.

Then he always asks,
"May I come in?"
And everyone says,
"How thoughtful of him!"

Think
What is the theme of this poem?

Bears Always Share

Bears share their toys.
Bears share their honey.
Bears share a joke
They think is funny.

Whatever they do,
Whatever they wear,
They always share it with
Another bear.

Think
What is the theme of this poem?

Understand

Comprehension

Think **What do you like about the poems? Check (✓). Why? Give one reason.**

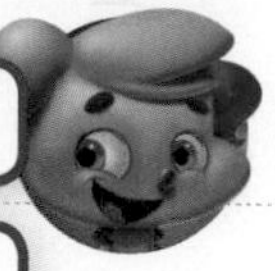 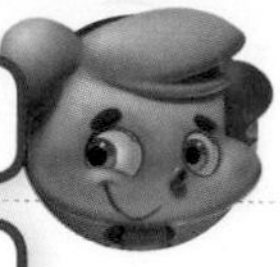 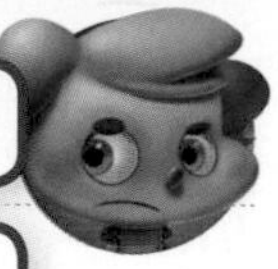

1 The raccoon poem	☐	☐	☐
2 The gorilla poem	☐	☐	☐
3 The ox poem	☐	☐	☐
4 The bear poem	☐	☐	☐

A Ask and answer the question.

What's your favorite part?

The gorilla poem. It's funny!

B Match the poems to the correct themes.

1 Welcome, Ricky Raccoon
2 Don't be Grabby, Gorilla
3 The Ox Always Knocks
4 Bears Always Share

a We should think about other people before we do something.
b We should help friends and get along with them.
c It's good to share our things with friends.
d It's good to be polite when we eat.

C Answer the questions.

1 Does Ricky Raccoon help his friends? ____________

2 What's one thing that bears share? ____________

Think **What do you think?**

1 Do Grabby Gorilla's friends like to play with him? Why or why not?
2 What is the theme of all the poems?

Workbook Grammar
pages 086–087

Grammar in Use

D **Listen and sing along.** **May I Come In?** 2•19

May I come in?
Yes, you may.
Thank you for
knocking.
Come in and play!

Can you please pass
That game to me?
Here you go.
We're friendly!

Don't be rude.
Please share your toys.
Be thoughtful of
Other girls and boys!

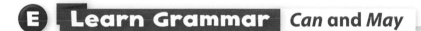

E **Learn Grammar** ***Can* and *May***

Can I play? Yes, you can. / No, you can't.
May I come in? Yes, you may. / No, you may not.

Role play with a partner. Use the words in the box or your own words.

watch TV	have a cookie	play outside	have some juice
go to my friend's house	go on the Internet		

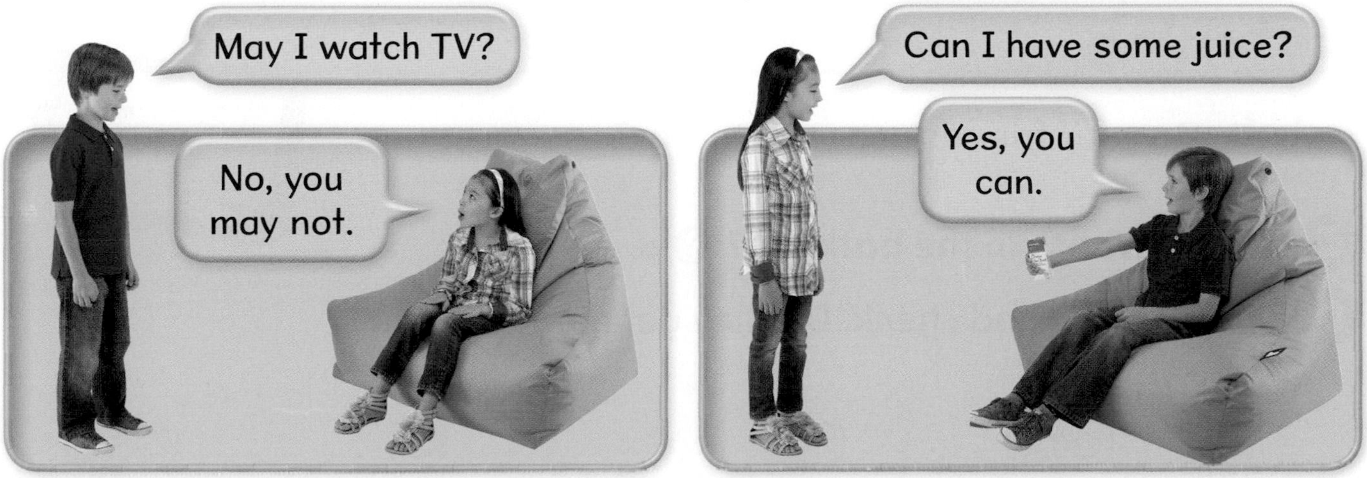

May I watch TV?
No, you may not.
Can I have some juice?
Yes, you can.

F **Tell your partner the things you need to ask to do at home. Which things are the same? Which things are different?**

Communicate

Words

A Listen and point to the words. Listen again and say the words. 2•20

computer	**laptop**	**camera**	**headphones**	**tablet**	**cell phone**

B Write the words from **A**.

1 We call and text our friends and families with this. ____________

2 We go on the Internet with this, but we don't often move it from place to place. ____________

3 We take pictures with this. ____________

4 This is smaller than a laptop. We can go on the Internet and play games with it. We don't open and close it. ____________

5 We put these on our ears and listen to music. ____________

6 We can go on the Internet and e-mail on this, and we can move it from place to place. ____________

Listening

Think Do your friends use your things?

C Listen. What's in the bath tub? 2•21

D Listen again and check. Do they get along? 2•22

1		
2		

3		
4		

Speaking

E **Take turns to ask for something in a polite way with your partner. Then act it out for the class. Use the words in the boxes to help.** 2•23

Are you using that computer?
Yes, I am. But we can share.
Great. Thanks.
Are you ...
May I ...
We can ...

Writing Study

F **Learn** Subject–Verb Agreement

When you're writing, check that you have the correct form of the verb.

He is careful with scissors and glue.

They were tired yesterday.

Read and circle the correct subject.

1 **Owen / The boys** were in the living room.

2 **I / We** am at school today.

3 **She / They** is very excited about the party.

4 **My test score / Their test scores** weren't very good.

Write **Tell your partner about a thoughtful person. Now write about him or her in your Workbook.** page 89

Wrap Up

A Listen and read along. 2•24

Project: Make a Rules Poster

B **Make a Rules Poster.**

- Write five of your own rules for the class to follow.
- Draw or find pictures.

C **Put your Rules Poster on the wall. Tell the class about one rule.**

Don't run around or talk in the library. Be polite to the librarian.

D **Walk around the room. Look at all the posters. Say one thing about each poster.**

I like this rule: Ask people to pass things. Don't grab.

My Rules Poster
1. Clean up your room and put away your things.
2. Share your things with your friends.
3. Always say "Please" and "thank you".
Thank you!
4. Don't run around or talk in the library.
5. Take turns on the play ground.

BIG QUESTION 5

How do people get along with each other?

A **Watch the video.**

B **Think more about the Big Question.**

C **Complete the Big Question Chart.**

What did you learn about how people get along with each other?

In units **11** and **12** you will:

WATCH a video about taking care of the Earth.

LEARN about the Earth's resources.

READ about a juice carton that gets recycled.

WRITE about natural resources you see every day.

MAKE a natural resource collage.

BIG QUESTION 6

Why should we take care of the Earth?

A **Watch the video.**

B **Look at the picture. What do you see?**

1 Where do you think this is?

2 What can people do here?

C **Think and answer the questions.**

1 Do you like to go outside?

2 Is the air in your town or city clean?

D **Fill out the Big Question Chart.**

What do you know about why we should take care of the Earth?

UNIT 11 Get Ready

Words

A Listen and point to the words. Listen again and say the words. 2•25

resources

wood

landfill

land

trash

smoke

sunlight

reduce

reuse

B Think about the words in **A** and add them to the chart.

Things people can do	Things people can make	Things people can't make
1	1 landfill	1
2	2	2
	3	3
		4

Before You Read

Think **What things do you need to live? What do you do with trash at school?**

C **Learn** **Main Idea and Details**

Remember, the main idea is what a text is about. The main idea is often the first sentence in a text. Details tell us more about the main idea.

Read the text. Answer the questions.

Rules in parks help to keep them clean and the animals safe.
Some rules are:

- Don't litter.
- Don't walk on the flowers.
- Clean up after eating.
- Don't give food to the birds or squirrels.

These rules keep everyone in the park safe and happy.

1 What is the main idea?

____

____

2 What are two details of the main idea?

____

____

D **Look at the pictures and captions on pages 110–111. What do you think the text is about?**

PREVIEW

Natural Resources

In this text, we learn about natural resources.

This text is an *informational text*. Remember, informational texts tell us about our world.

Earth Science

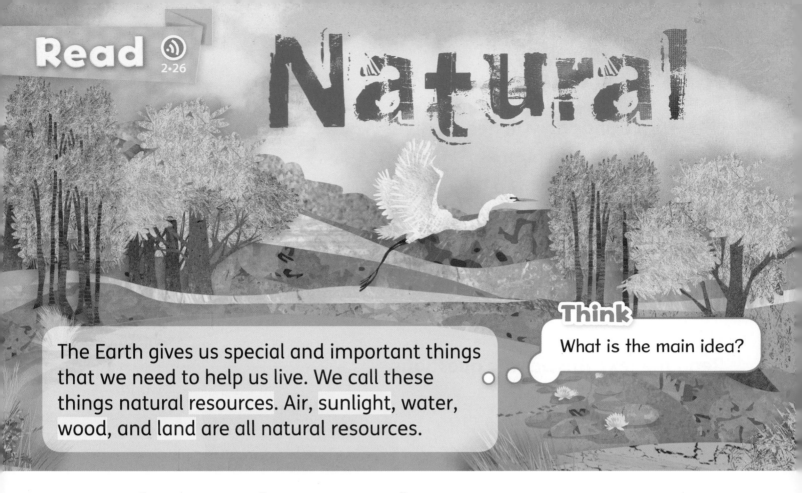

Read 2•26

Natural

The Earth gives us special and important things that we need to help us live. We call these things natural resources. Air, sunlight, water, wood, and land are all natural resources.

Think

What is the main idea?

People Need Natural Resources

Living things need clean air to breathe and clean water to drink. Plants need sunlight and land to grow, and we need plants for food. When plants breathe, they clean the air around them. We use the wood from plants and trees to make a lot of things, like paper, some houses, and furniture.

Hurting Our Natural Resources

We shouldn't hurt our natural resources because we can't usually make more of them. Smoke from cars and factories makes the air dirty. If the air is dirty, people can get sick and plants can't grow. If we cut down trees, we should plant new ones.

Trash is very bad for our natural resources. Sometimes people throw trash into water but we can't drink dirty water, and plants can't grow near it.

Trash goes to places called landfills, and it stays there forever. Some landfills are dirty and they smell bad. People can't use that land, and farmers can't grow food on it.

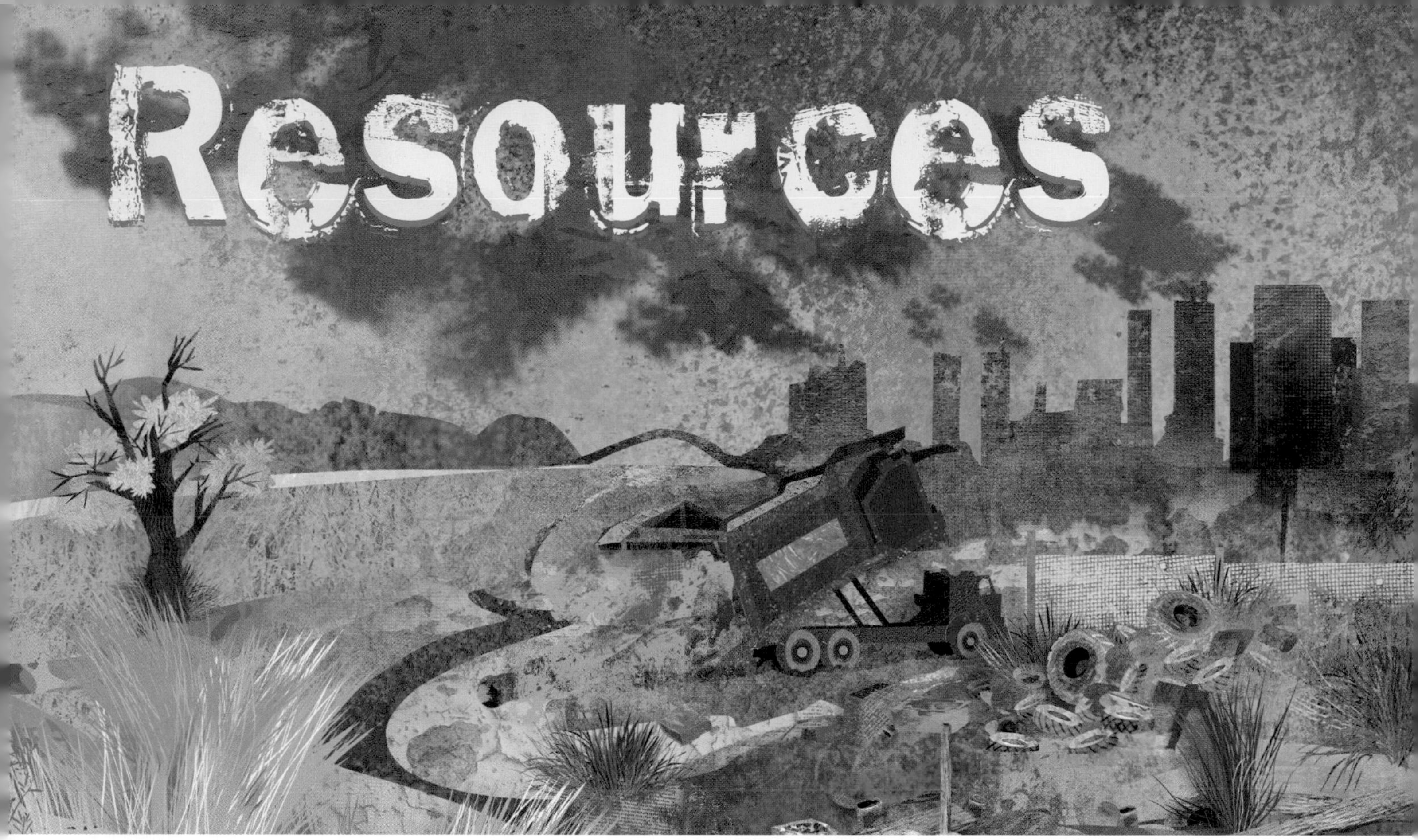

Taking Care of Our Natural Resources

We can all take care of the Earth's resources. Here are some ideas:

- Use things until you can't use them anymore.
- Don't throw things away. Reuse them. Refill plastic drink bottles. Make toys from old things.
- Reduce the natural resources you use. Take your own bag to the store.

Think

Find one detail of the main idea.

What can you do today to help take care of our natural resources?

Understand

Comprehension

Think **What do you like about the text? Check (✓). Why? Give one reason.**

1 Different natural resources	☐	☐	☐
2 Why we need natural resources	☐	☐	☐
3 How we hurt natural resources	☐	☐	☐
4 How we can take care of natural resources	☐	☐	☐

A **Ask and answer the question.**

What's your favorite part?

How I can reuse things. I can help the Earth.

B **Look back at the paragraph "People need natural resources." Answer the questions.**

1 What is the main idea? ____________________

2 What are two details? ____________________

____

C **Answer the questions.**

1 Why should we take care of the Earth's natural resources? ____________________

____

2 What makes the air dirty? ____________________

Think **What do you think?**

1 When do people use natural resources?

2 What can people do to reduce trash?

Grammar in Use

D Listen and sing along. **The Tree** 2•27

Behind the house
There is a tree.
It grows peaches
Just for me.

Between the flowers
There's a bee.
It flies around
In front of me.

Across from me,
The eagles fly,
Above the ground,
Into the sky.

E **Learn Grammar** Prepositions of Place

There's smoke in the air above the city.
The landfill is across from the park.

The trash can is behind the tree.
The tree is in front of the trash can.

Where are all the things in the park? Practice with a partner.

There are birds above the pond.
There are trees behind the pond.

F **Look around your classroom. Say where things are. Practice with your partner.**

Communicate

Words

A Listen and point to the words. Listen again and say the words. 2•28

camp

hike

ride a horse

surf

fish

ski

B One of the words is incorrect. Cross out the wrong answer.

1	You need an animal to do this.	a **ride a horse**	b ~~**hike**~~
2	You do this in the ocean.	a **ski**	b **surf**
3	You go down the mountain very fast.	a **camp**	b **ski**
4	You can sit in a boat to do this.	a **fish**	b **surf**

Listening

Think Do you ever go camping?

C Listen. Where is the pollution? 2•29

D Listen again and number the activities in the order you hear them. Then circle *can* or *can't*. 2•30

☐ camp	can	can't		1 fish	can	(can't)
☐ ski	can	can't		☐ ride a horse	can	can't
☐ surf	can	can't		☐ hike	can	can't

Speaking

E **Listen and repeat. Then practice with a partner. Use the words in the box to help.** 2•31

I apologize.
I'm very sorry.
behind
near
there it is

Word Study

F **Learn** Verbs, Nouns, Adjectives, and Pronouns

Remember, a **verb** is an action word. A **noun** is a person, place, or thing. An **adjective** tells more about a noun. A **pronoun** takes the place of a noun.

Verb: reduce **Noun:** trash **Adjective:** healthy **Pronoun:** they

Write verb, noun, adjective, or pronoun for the highlighted words.

1 The clever little monkey (noun) stole bananas from us.

2 Mandy wrote a long letter to her grandmother.

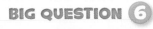

Tell your partner about three natural resources you see every day.
Write **Now write about them in your Workbook.** page 99

BIG QUESTION 6

Why should we take care of the Earth?

I think trash is bad for our natural resources.
I think we need clean air to breathe.

UNIT 12 Get Ready

Words

A Listen and point to the words. Listen again and say the words. 2•32

carton

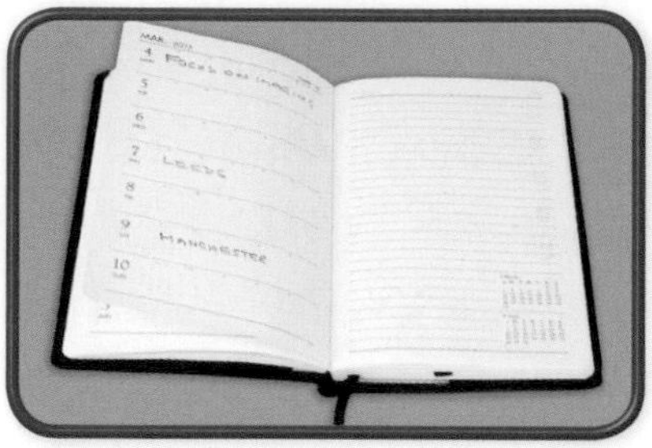

diary

paper

blow

shelf

recycling plant

machine

stationery store

rescue

B Think about the words in **A** and add them to the chart.

Places	Things	Things People Can Do
1 recycling plant	1	1
2	2	2
	3	
	4	
	5	

Before You Read

Think What do you do with clothes that are too small? What does your family reuse?

C **Learn** Setting

Setting is the place where the story happens. It answers the question *Where*? Knowing where the story takes place helps you understand more about the story.

A Grade 2 class brings newspapers, bottles, and cans to the classroom to recycle.

Setting: School

Read the story. Circle the correct setting.

Antonio and his dad are in a beautiful place. They're looking at some trees and birds.

Antonio's dad says, "People cut down too many trees and don't plant new ones. Then there aren't enough trees for animals to make homes in. We need to take care of Earth's resources."

Setting: **Rainforest** / **Beach**

D **The story on pages 118–119 is about a juice carton that gets recycled. What do you think it gets recycled into?**

A Juice Carton's Diary

This story is *narrative fiction*. In narrative fiction, a character tells a story that the author has made up.

Beth Cody Kimmel is a children's book writer. She lives in New York.

Read 2•33

A Juice Carton's Diary

January 15

Dear Diary,
I'm sitting on a shelf in a big store! I can see many wonderful things. The little carton in front of me has a picture of an orange on it. I think I know what I am. I'm an orange juice carton! I'm made of hard paper.

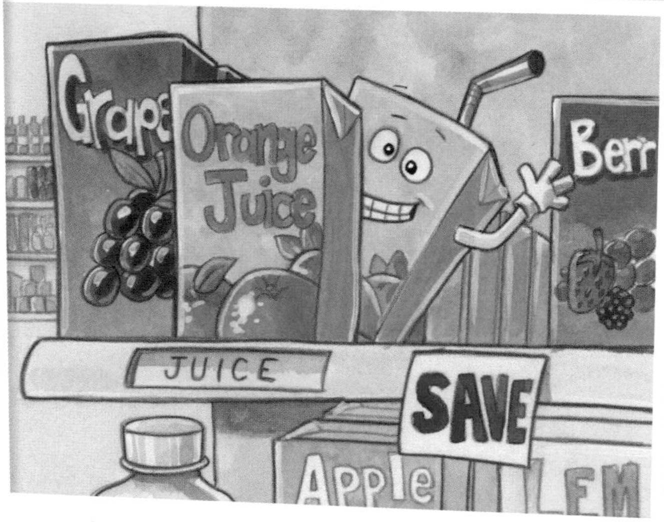

January 16

Dear Diary,
This morning something great happened. A little girl looked at my shelf for a long time, and then she chose me! She's taking me to a picnic by the lake so I hope she's very thirsty.

January 17

Dear Diary,
I'm in a lake! The little girl drank the juice, but she left me in front of the lake. The wind blew me into the water. I don't like it here. There was a trash can behind the tree. Why didn't the little girl put me in it?

Think
Where is the juice carton?

January 18

Dear Diary,
I saw a man taking litter out of the lake with a net. He saw my bright orange carton, and he rescued me! He caught me and a plastic bottle in his net. Now we're in the boat, and we aren't trash anymore! We're happy.

January 19

Dear Diary,
I'm at the recycling plant! It's a little scary here because there are large machines that make loud noises. Where's my plastic bottle friend? He's across from me. He's in a bin with other plastic bottles. I think this is a good place.

Think
Where is the juice carton?

January 20

Dear Diary,
I'm sitting on a shelf in a stationery store! Everything here is made of paper! Yes, they recycled me into a notebook! I'm very happy and excited, and I really want to see the recycling plant again. Maybe next time I'll be a comic book!

Understand

Comprehension

Think **What do you like about the story? Check (✓). Why? Give one reason.**

1 The girl buys the carton of juice.	☐	☐	☐
2 The man on the lake	☐	☐	☐
3 The carton in the recycling plant	☐	☐	☐
4 The carton is now a notebook.	☐	☐	☐

A Ask and answer the question.

What's your favorite part?

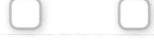

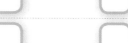

The carton was recycled into a notebook. That's interesting.

B Answer the questions.

1 How many settings are in the story? ______

2 Name each setting: ______

C Number the events in the correct order.

☐ The girl took the juice carton to a lake.

☐ The juice carton felt a little scared.

1 The juice carton sat on a shelf in the store.

☐ The juice carton was recycled into a notebook.

☐ A man rescued the carton with a net.

Think **What do you think?**

1 What other things can a juice carton be recycled into?

2 Why is it important to recycle things?

Grammar in Use

D Listen and sing along. **Where is Charlie?** 2•34

I'm looking for my cat Charlie.
He ran away from me.
Where is my cat Charlie?
Come and look with me.

Is he under the trash can,
Between the bench and the tree?
No, he isn't. He isn't there.
Oh, where can Charlie be?

Is he over there in the fountain,
Across from the big statue?
Yes, he is! Poor Charlie!
I'm here to rescue you!

E **Learn Grammar** Prepositions of Place

Where's the fountain? It's across from the statue.
Is there a trash can behind the tree? Yes, there is.

Where is it? Look at the picture and practice with a partner.

Is there a bicycle in front of the red bin?
Trash Can
No, there isn't. There's a bicycle next to the green bin.

F Look for three things. Ask your partner where they are.

Communicate

Words

A **Listen and point to the words. Listen again and say the words.** 2•35

time

week

nine o'clock / 9:00

nine-fifteen / 9:15

nine-thirty / 9:30

nine forty-five / 9:45

B **Circle the correct word or times.**

1 There are seven days in a **time** / **week** .

2 Mia goes to school at **7:30** / **2:30** in the morning.

3 The girls go to bed at **3:00** / **9:00** at night.

4 What **week** / **time** did you see the doctor? At 4:00.

5 We usually come home from school at **3:15** / **8:15** in the afternoon.

6 My mother cooks dinner at **5:30** / **11:30** in the evening.

Listening

Think **What days do they pick up trash in your neighborhood?**

C **Listen. What did Lucas do after lunch?** 2•36

D **Listen again and circle the correct times.** 2•37

1	7:00	11:30	4	1:45	1:00
2	9:15	9:30	5	2:00	3:00
3	10:45	10:00	6	2:15	2:30

Speaking

E **What did you do last week to help keep the Earth clean? Find a partner who did the same thing. Use the words in the boxes to help.** 2•38

Writing Study

F **Learn** Verb Tenses to Show Time

Verbs show the time of an action.

Look at the verb **go**.

I go to school.

I'm going to school.

I went to school.

go: usually happens

going: happening now

went: already happened

Write the correct verb form to complete the sentence.

1 We ___ate___ cookies in the park this morning. (eat)

2 Lisa is ______________ her trash in the trash can. (throw)

3 I usually ______________ the paper in that bin. (reuse)

4 The students are ______________ trees near the playground now. (plant)

Write **Imagine you are something that was recycled. What were you? What are you now? Tell a partner. Now write about it in your Workbook.** page 107

Wrap Up

A Listen and read along. 2•39

Gus's family is getting ready for their vacation.
Clean this room or you can't come!
Gus throws his trash into the trash can.
Help me, Dot!
OK. You can reuse this!
They recycle paper, plastic bottles, and cartons.
You can recycle that.
Oh, OK.
They give clothes away so someone can reuse them.
You can give those to our cousin.
They're on vacation. Gus and his family camp in the woods.
Look at the sunlight!
It's wonderful here!
They fish and ride horses. They have a great time.
Let's keep the Earth clean!
TRASH

Project: Make a Natural Resource Collage

B **Make a natural resource collage.**

- Why is this natural resource important?
- Draw or find pictures.
- Write about three things in the collage.

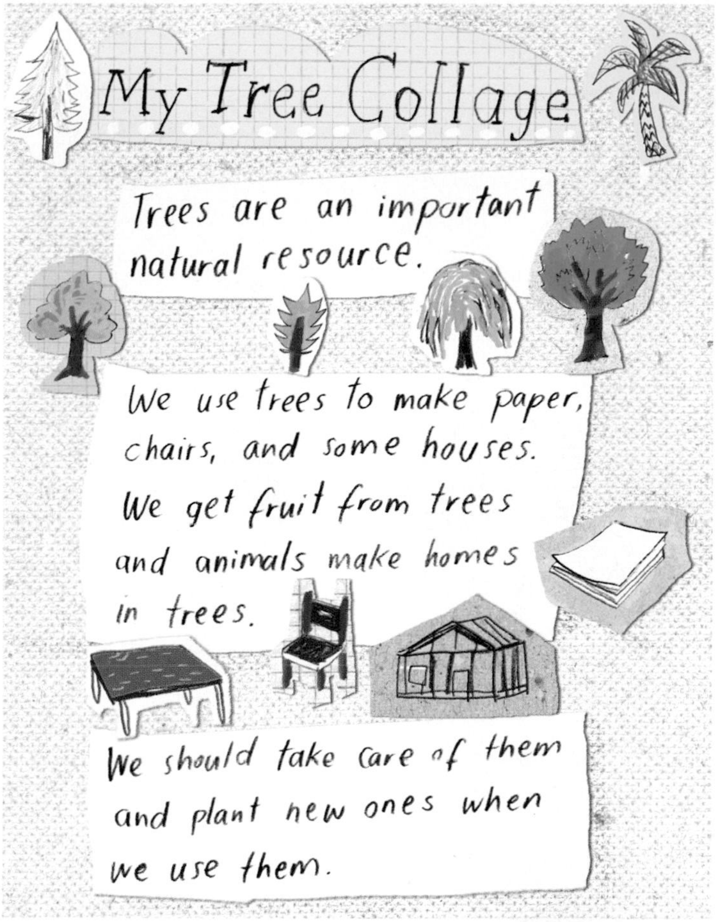

My Tree Collage
Trees are an important natural resource.
We use trees to make paper, chairs, and some houses. We get fruit from trees and animals make homes in trees.
We should take care of them and plant new ones when we use them.

C **Put your collage on the wall. Tell the class about your collage.**

This is my tree collage. Trees are an important natural resource. We make paper, chairs, and houses from trees.

D **Walk around the room. Look at the collages. Say one thing about each collage.**

I learned that sunlight helps the plants grow.

BIG QUESTION 6

Why should we take care of the Earth?

A **Watch the video.**

B **Think more about the Big Question.**

C Complete the **Big Question Chart.**

What did you learn about why we should take care of the Earth?

In units **13** and **14** you will:

WATCH a video about music.

LEARN about music and feelings.

READ about a concert.

WRITE about how a piece of music made you feel.

MAKE a music mobile.

BIG QUESTION 7

How does music make us feel?

A **Watch the video.**

B **Look at the picture. What do you see?**

1 What is the girl doing?

2 How do you think she feels?

C **Think and answer the questions.**

1 Can you play a musical instrument?

2 What's your favorite kind of music?

D **Fill out the Big Question Chart.**

What do you know about music?
BIG QUESTION Chart

Get Ready

Words

A Listen and point to the words. Listen again and say the words. 2•40

high

low

excited

sleepy

wolf

feelings

right

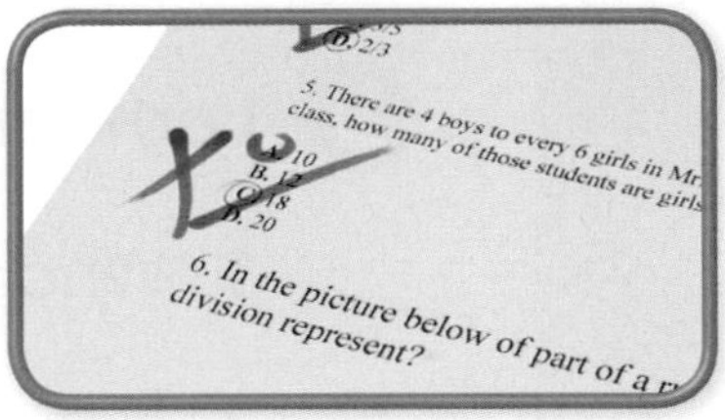

wrong

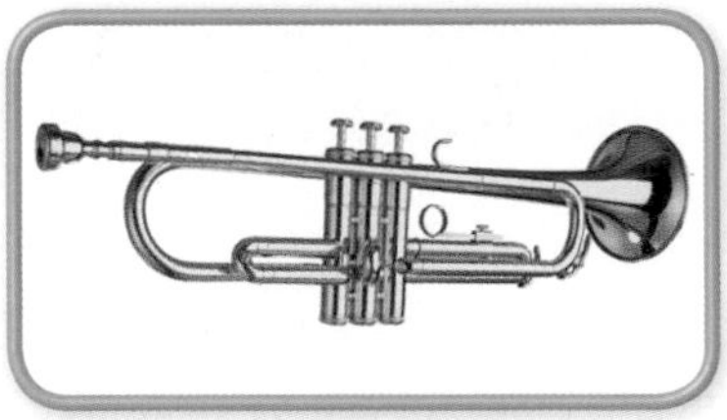

trumpet

B Complete the sentences. Circle the two correct words.

1 Music can be …
a high
b wrong
c low

2 I listen to music and I sometimes feel …
a sleepy
b right
c excited

3 His answers to the math problems were …
a high
b right
c wrong

4 In the concert she played …
a a drum
b a trumpet
c high

5 A dog is similar to …
a a fox
b a lizard
c a wolf

6 She is feeling ….
a happy
b excited
c trumpet

Before You Read

Think What's your favorite song? Do you like fast or slow music?

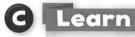

C **Learn** Summarize

To summarize, we tell the most important parts of the text. We don't use a lot of words, and we don't tell a lot of the details.

Children all over the world play musical instruments. They can have a lot of different feelings when they play. In the beginning, a lot of them feel excited. But then they need to practice every day, and sometimes they think music is boring.

Summary: Children can have a lot of different feelings when they play musical instruments.

Read the text. Then circle the correct summary.

There are a lot of different instruments in a band in a parade. The drums, cymbals, and trumpets can be loud. Some children feel excited when they hear loud music, but some children feel scared.

Summary:

1 Some children feel excited when they hear loud music in a parade. Some feel scared.

2 People at parades all feel excited, scared, and happy.

D **The text on pages 130–131 is about music and feelings. What are three words you think are in the text?**

PREVIEW

How Music Makes Us Feel

In this text we learn about music and how it makes us feel.

This text is an *informational text*. Remember, informational texts tell us about our world.

Music

Read 2•41

How Music Makes Us Feel

Pedro listens to slow music at night so he can fall asleep.

People all around the world enjoy music. Some music is fast, and some music is slow. Some music is high, and some music is low. Listen to this piano music. What can you say about it? Is it fast or slow, high or low?

Music and Feelings

When we listen to music, we feel different things. Slow music can make us feel sleepy, and fast music can make us feel excited. The same music can make one person feel sad and another person feel happy. There are no right or wrong feelings about music.

Listen to this flute music. How does it make you feel? Mothers play this music for their babies at night because it helps the babies sleep. Now listen to this trumpet music. How does it make you feel?

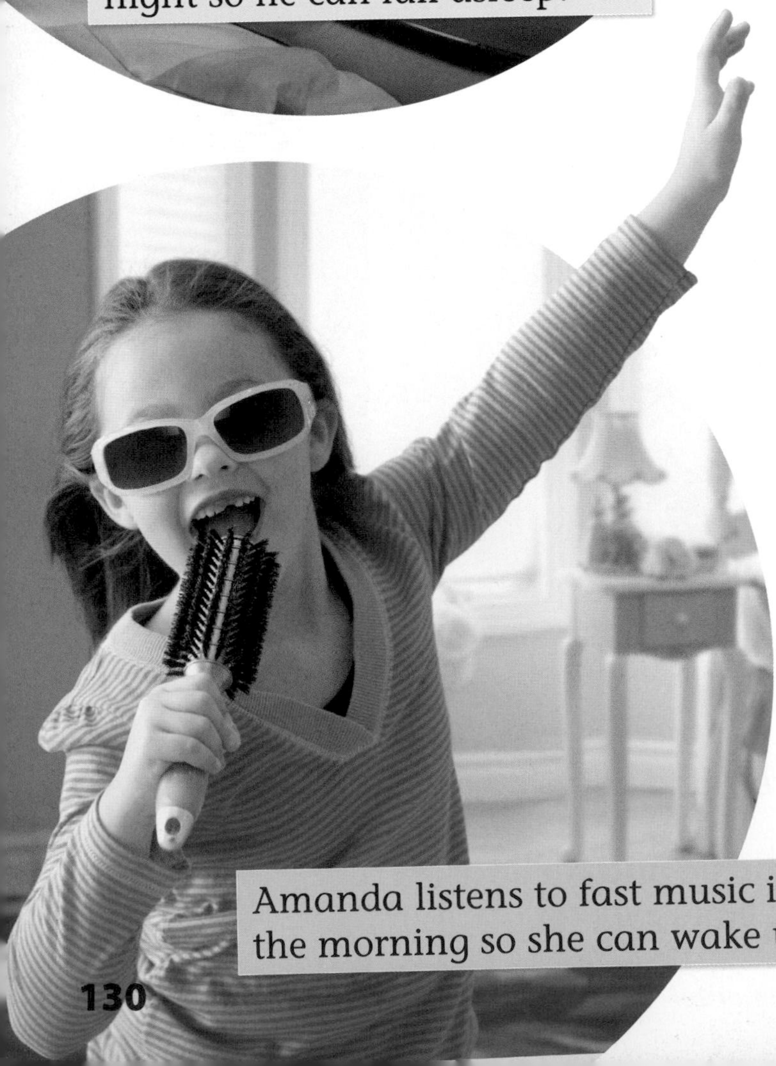

Amanda listens to fast music in the morning so she can wake up.

Think

What are the most important parts so far?

Music and Imagination

Music can help us imagine things, like animals. When the music is fast, we can imagine an animal running. When it's slow, we can imagine an animal sleeping. When it's low and slow, we can imagine an animal that is in danger. Listen. What animal does this sound like, a duck or a wolf? What do you imagine the animals are doing?

Listen to this music. What did you hear, thunder or rain? Now listen again. What did you hear this time?

Next time you listen to music, draw a picture of what you imagine. Look at it a week later. Does it help you to remember the music?

Think

What are the most important parts so far?

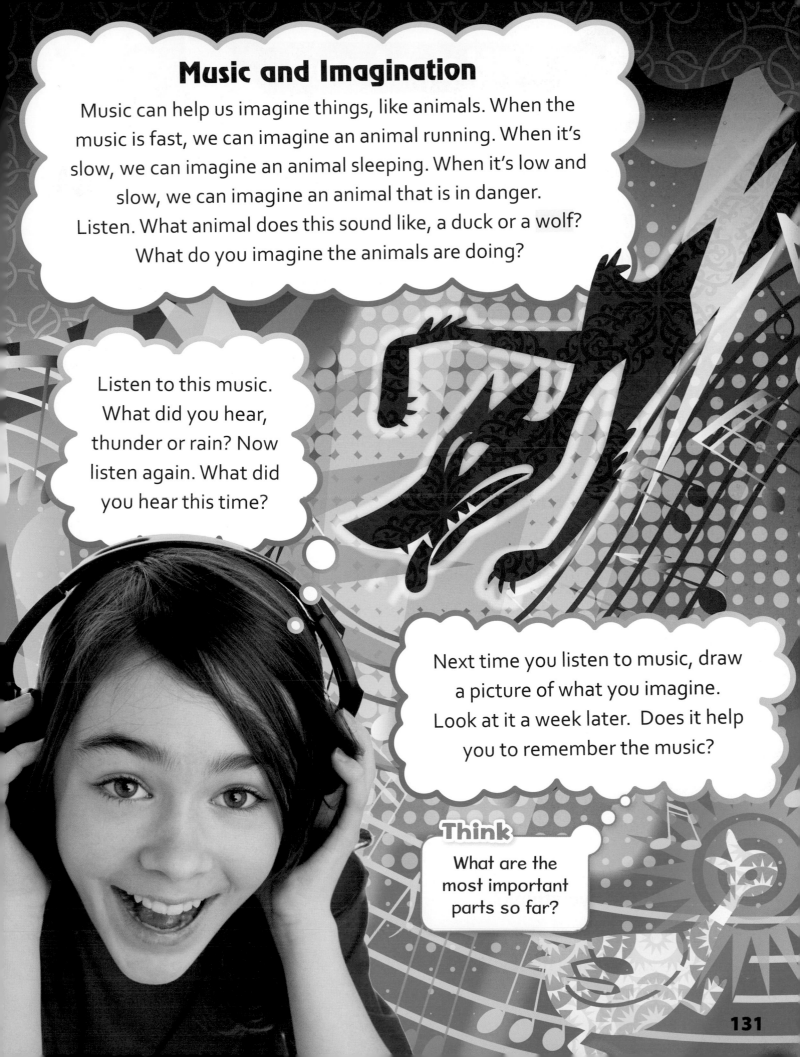

Understand

Comprehension

Think **What do you like about the text? Check (✓). Why? Give one reason.**

1 The different sounds of music	☐	☐	☐
2 How music makes us feel	☐	☐	☐
3 Music helps us imagine things.	☐	☐	☐

A **Ask and answer the question.**

What's your favorite part?

The music. I could imagine the animals.

B **Circle the correct answer.**

1 All music sounds the same.	True	False
2 People have the same feelings when they listen to music.	True	False
3 Music helps us imagine a lot of different things.	True	False
4 The music about bees was fast.	True	False

C **Think of the most important parts of the text. Summarize the text.**

Music makes people feel …

Think **What do you think?**

1 How does music make us have different feelings?

2 We want to feel happy. What kind of music should we listen to?

Grammar in Use

D **Listen and sing along.** **Music Day!** 2•42

In the morning when
Gus gets ready for
school,

He likes fast music …
it's so cool!

He likes guitars and
drums the best,

While he brushes his
teeth and gets dressed!

On Monday he goes to
school with friends.

In music class, he plays
instruments.

The high flute notes
sound like birds in a
tree,

The low trombone, like
whales in the sea!

He doesn't listen
to loud music
at night.

He listens to music
that's soft and light,

Like the violin, when
he rests his head,

Closes his eyes
and goes to bed.

E **Learn Grammar** **Prepositions of Time**

Pedro listens to slow music **at night**.

When does Amanda listen to slow music?

She listens **in** the **morning.**

Choose one of the girls. Your partner asks questions to guess.

in the morning | in the afternoon | in the evening

Saturday

Sandy	Imani
Morning: practice the piano	Morning: practice the piano
Afternoon: lunch with Grandma	Afternoon: lunch with Mom and Dad
Evening: trumpet lesson	Evening: dance lesson

Does she go to her trumpet lesson in the evening?

Yes, she does.

It's Sandy.

F **Ask your partner about Saturdays.**

What do you do in the morning?

Communicate

Words

A Listen and point to the words. Listen again and say the words. 2•43

proud

smile

nervous

yawn

unhappy

cry

B Think about the words in **A** and add them to the chart.

Feelings	Actions
1 proud	1
2	2
3	3

Listening

Think When do you get nervous?

C Listen. Why are the students practicing music? 2•44

D Listen again and match. 2•45

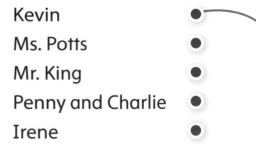

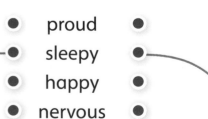

Kevin	proud	smile
Ms. Potts	sleepy	cry
Mr. King	happy	yawn
Penny and Charlie	nervous	clap
Irene	unhappy	run away

Speaking

E Listen and repeat. Then practice with a partner. Use the words in the box to help. 2•46

that song
the radio
that CD
hate
can't stand
I love it.
I think it's great.

Word Study

F **Learn** Synonyms

Some words mean the same thing. These words are called **synonyms**.

happy → glad   **trash** → garbage

Match the words.

close
tired
strike
noisy

1 shut

2 sleepy

3 loud

4 hit

Write Think about a piece of music. Tell your partner about how it made you feel. Now write about it in your **Workbook**. page 117

BIG QUESTION 7

How does music make us feel?

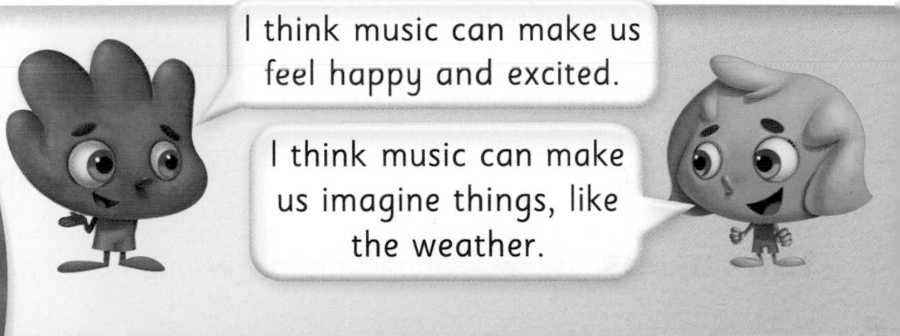

I think music can make us feel happy and excited.
I think music can make us imagine things, like the weather.

UNIT 14 Get Ready

Words

A Listen and point to the words. Listen again and say the words. 3•02

notes

wait

worried

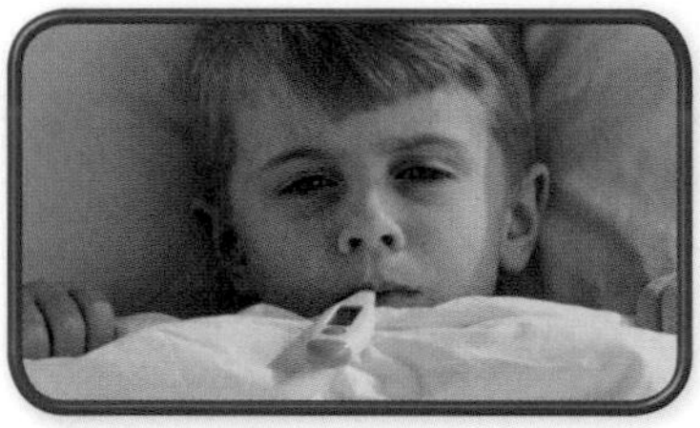

the flu

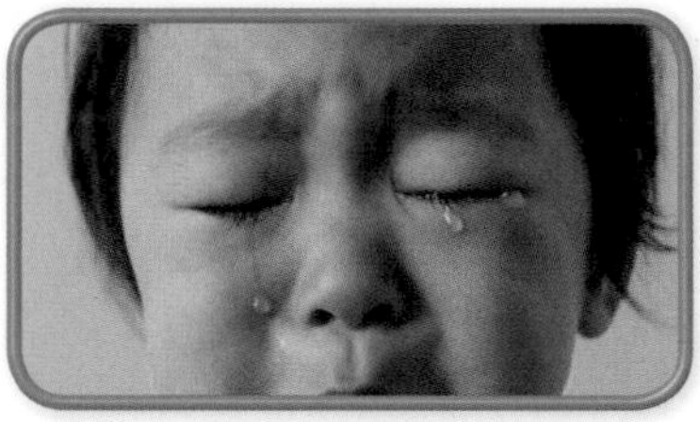

tears

solo

hummingbird

record

musician

B Write the words to complete the sentences.

1 This ________________ has beautiful feathers.

2 I sometimes ________________ a long time for the train.

3 When a ________________ plays an instrument alone, he or she plays a ________________.

4 ________________ come out of our eyes when we cry.

5 Musicians often look at ________________ on paper when they play.

6 I am often ________________ before an important test.

7 When people get ________________ they feel awful.

8 We ________________ songs so that we can listen to them later.

Before You Read

Think **Does your school have concerts? What's your favorite musical instrument?**

C Learn Characters

All stories have characters. Characters are the people, animals, or things that are in the story. There are main characters and secondary characters.

Main characters are the most important characters. The story is about them.

Secondary characters aren't as important as the main characters.

Laura and her baby sister, Clara, are listening to some soft and slow music. Laura loves the low notes. She feels calm. Clara falls asleep.

Main character: Laura **Secondary character:** Clara

Read the story. Write the names of the characters.

Sammy plays the trumpet but he doesn't like to practice. He plays a piece of music for his teacher, Mr. Green. The music is loud and awful. His teacher is unhappy. Sammy practices every day now.

1 Main character: ______________

2 Secondary character: ______________

D The title of the story is "Olga's Flute." How do you think Olga feels when she plays her instrument?

PREVIEW

Olga's Flute

This story is realistic fiction. *Realistic fiction* is a story that isn't true, but it could happen.

Beth Cody Kimmel is a children's book writer. She lives in New York.

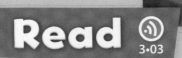

Read 3•03

Olga's Flute

When Olga plays her flute she feels many things. High and slow notes make her feel happy and the low long notes can make her feel sleepy. When Olga plays a fast tune, she feels like she is flying.

Olga's school is having a big concert tonight. Olga plays second flute, so if the first flute player gets sick, Olga can play his or her part.

Think

Which character is in this part of the story?

Today Olga goes to school early for extra practice. Her music teacher is waiting for her.

"Alonso has the flu," Mr. Perez tells Olga. "You must play his part tonight."

Olga is very worried. "Alonso is the best flute player in the school," she says. "I'm not good enough."

Mr. Perez smiles. "You practice every day, Olga," he tells her. "Alonso plays well, but so do you. Please try, Olga."

Think

Which character is in this part of the story?

She closes her eyes and begins to play, but this morning she feels nervous. The high notes are hard to reach and the fast notes are difficult to play. The quiet part seems too loud. When Olga finishes, her eyes fill with tears.

"I wish I could play like Alonso," she says.

Mr. Perez pushes a button on his computer and Olga hears music. She thinks it is Alonso's flute solo. She imagines butterflies on the high notes. The fast notes sound like hummingbirds or rain. The low, quiet notes are like snow falling. "That's beautiful. I wish I played liked that!" Olga says.

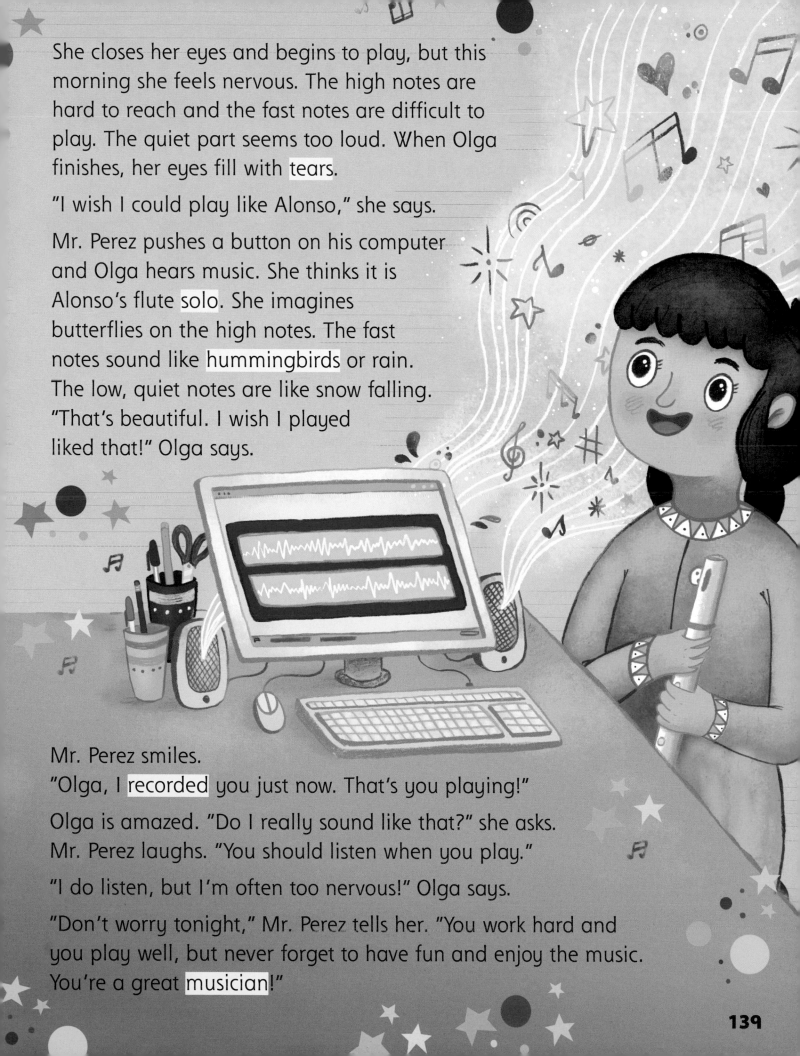

Mr. Perez smiles.
"Olga, I recorded you just now. That's you playing!"

Olga is amazed. "Do I really sound like that?" she asks. Mr. Perez laughs. "You should listen when you play."

"I do listen, but I'm often too nervous!" Olga says.

"Don't worry tonight," Mr. Perez tells her. "You work hard and you play well, but never forget to have fun and enjoy the music. You're a great musician!"

Understand

Comprehension

Think **What do you like about the story? Check (✓). Why? Give one reason.**

1 How Olga feels when she plays her flute	☐	☐	☐
2 Mr. Perez records Olga.	☐	☐	☐
3 Olga knows that Mr. Perez recorded her music.	☐	☐	☐

A **Ask and answer the question.**

What's your favorite part?

Mr. Perez plays Olga's music on his computer. I like that.

B **Answer the questions.**

1 Who is the main character? ______________

2 Who are the secondary characters? ______________ ______________

C **Answer the questions.**

1 What notes make Olga feel happy? ______________

2 Why does Olga have to play Alonso's part at the concert? ______________

3 Does Olga think she plays Alonso's part well? ______________

4 Does Mr. Perez think Olga plays Alonso's part well? ______________

Think **What do you think?**

1 Is Mr. Perez smart and kind? Why? Why not?

2 How does Olga play at the concert?

Grammar in Use

D Listen and sing along. **The Concert** 3-04

Gus plays lots of instruments.
He practices each day.
He makes amazing music.
It's great to hear him play!

Last week Gus played the cymbals.
And then played the guitar.
Yesterday he played the trumpet.
His friends think he's a star.

Last night he played the piano.
And then played the drum.
This morning he played the tambourine.
He had a lot of fun.

E **Learn Grammar** Adverbs of Time

This morning, Olga goes to school early for extra practice.

When did Mark go to music class?

He went **yesterday morning**.

Who is it? Ask and answer questions with your partner.

Name	Last Week	Yesterday Morning	Yesterday Afternoon	Last Night
 Mike				
 Tim				

Did he practice the piano last week?

Yes, he did.

It's Mike!

Key: practice the piano  listen to music 

F Tell your partner something you did yesterday and today.

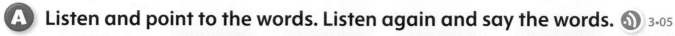

Communicate

Words

A Listen and point to the words. Listen again and say the words. 3•05

have lunch

give a concert

make a mistake

sign an autograph

talk to fans

do an interview

B Cross out the wrong answer.

1 The popstar uses a pen to do this.
a **talk to fans** b **sign an autograph**

2 Mia and Bea do this at 12:00 every day.
a **have lunch** b **give a concert**

3 I don't like it when I do this. It makes me angry.
a **make a mistake** b **have lunch**

4 The teacher wants her class to do this with instruments.
a **do an interview** b **give a concert**

Listening

Think Are there concerts in your town?

C Listen. What does Cameron do? 3•06

D Listen again and number the activities in the order you hear them. Circle the feeling. 3•07

☐	gave a concert	unhappy	nervous
☐	did an interview	tired	excited
☐	signed autographs	proud	happy
1	made a mistake	calm	(unhappy)

Speaking

E **Imagine you're a musician. Tell your partner something you did and how you felt. Use the words in the boxes to help.** 3•08

Writing Study

F **Learn** Using *And* and *But*

We can put two sentences together to make one sentence. We use **and** when the ideas are similar and **but** when they are not.

I'm singing. I'm playing the piano.
I'm singing and I'm playing the piano.

Aden is excited. I'm nervous.
Aden is excited, but I'm nervous.

Use *and* or *but* to make one sentence.

1 I can play the low notes. I can't play the high notes.
I can play the low notes, but I can't play the high notes.

2 He talks to fans. He signs autographs.
____

3 We went to a concert. We didn't go to a ballet.
____

Write **Tell your partner about your favorite music and what it sounds like. Now write about it in your Workbook.** page 125

Units 13 and 14

Wrap Up

A Listen and read along. 3•09

Project: Make a Music Mobile

B Make a music mobile.

- Choose five things about music.
- Write your feelings about them.
- Draw or find pictures.

I don't like trumpets. They make me feel nervous.
I like flutes. They make me feel calm.
Low notes make me feel sleepy
Parade music makes me feel excited.

C Hang your music mobile in the room. Tell the class about one of the pictures on your mobile.

I like parades. The music makes me feel excited.

D Walk around the room. Find one mobile that's the same as yours and one that's different.

Ben likes trumpet music, but I don't. He feels excited, but I feel nervous. Carrie and I like flute music because it makes us feel calm.

BIG QUESTION 7

How does music make us feel?

A Watch the video.

B Think more about the Big Question.

C Complete the **Big Question Chart**.

What did you learn about how music makes us feel?

In units **15** and **16** you will:

WATCH a video about forces and movement.

LEARN about forces and movement.

READ about two goats who didn't get along.

WRITE about things you push and pull.

MAKE a forces poster.

BIG QUESTION 8

What makes things move?

A Watch the video.

B Look at the picture. What do you see?

1 Where are they?

2 What are they doing?

C Think and answer the questions.

1 Can a car move by itself?

2 What things move slowly?

D Fill out the **Big Question Chart**.

What do you know about what makes things move?
BIG QUESTION Chart

UNIT 15 Get Ready

Words

A Listen and point to the words. Listen again and say the words. 3•10

push

pull

movement

ground

throw

speed

heavy

light

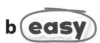

easy

B Circle the correct word.

1 I did the math problems quickly. They were very … — a **long** b **easy**

2 The horse is fast. The tortoise can't chase it, because the … of the tortoise is too slow. — a **speed** b **movement**

3 The farmers … carrots out of the ground. — a **push** b **pull**

4 Birds' feathers are very … — a **heavy** b **light**

5 Farmers grow food in the … — a **landfill** b **ground**

6 The boy ... the ball to his friend. — a **throws** b **catches**

Before You Read

Think How far can you kick a ball? Can you pick up a big table?

C **Learn** Cause and Effect

Remember, a **cause** is why something happens.

The **effect** is what happens after the cause.

Read the text. Write the causes and effects.

Chicks can't fly when they are very small, so parent birds get food for them. Chicks move their wings in the nest. Their wings get strong and when they get big, they leave the nest. They move their wings up and down and fly in the air.

Cause	Effect
1 Chicks can't fly.	a
2	b Their wings get strong.
3	c They leave the nest.
4 They move their wings up and down.	d

D **Look at the title and headings on pages 150–151. What do you think the text is about?**

PREVIEW

Forces and MOVEMENT

This text is an *informational text*. Remember, informational texts tell us about our world.

Physical Science

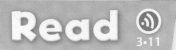

Read 3•11

Forces and MOVEMENT

We see things move every day. We see people walking, birds flying, and leaves falling to the ground on a windy day. Things move in many ways. They move up and down, right and left, and over and under things. Look around your classroom. What things are moving?

Force

A force makes something move. A push is a force, and it moves something away from you. We push people on swings. A pull is a force, too, and it moves something toward you. We pull things in wagons. Can you name something you push and something you pull?

Think

What's the cause of the wagon moving?
What's the effect of the girl pulling the wagon?

MOVEMENT

A small force causes a small movement and a big force causes a big movement. When we use a small force to throw a ball, it doesn't go far. When we use a big force to throw the same ball, it goes a long way.

It is easier to move a light thing than a heavy thing. We can move a toy car with a small force because it's light. We need a big force to move a real car because it's heavy.

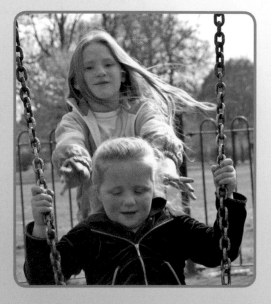

Speed

Speed is how fast things move. Some things, like a train, move fast and some things, like a tortoise, move slowly. Can you name some things that move fast?

A force can change the speed of things. When you push a door with a small force, it opens slowly, but when you push a door with a big force, it opens quickly.

Think

What's the cause of the door opening slowly? What's the effect of the door being pushed with a small force?

The next time you see something moving, ask yourself, "What force is moving it, a push or a pull? Is the force small or big?"

Understand

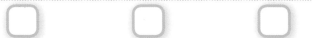

Comprehension

Think **What do you like about the text? Check (✓). Why? Give one reason.**

1 How force makes things move	☐	☐	☐
2 Big and small forces cause different movements.	☐	☐	☐
3 How force changes speed	☐	☐	☐

A **Ask and answer the question.**

What's your favorite part?

Heavy things need a big force to move them. I didn't know that.

B **Complete the chart. Write the cause or effect.**

Cause	Effect
1 We push something.	a
2	b There is a small movement.
3 We open a door with a big force.	c

C **Circle the correct answer.**

1 A force doesn't make things move. True False

2 Push and pull are forces. True False

3 A light object needs a big force to move it. True False

4 A force can change the speed of things. True False

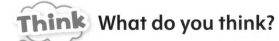

Think **What do you think?**

1 What is heavy and needs a big force to move it?

2 Is it easier to push your father or your friend on a swing? Why?

Workbook Grammar
pages 132–133

Grammar in Use

D Listen and sing along. **The Horse, the Tortoise, and Me** 3•12

A horse is faster than a tortoise,
And a horse is faster than me.
I'm slower than a horse,
So what is slower than me?

A horse is bigger than a tortoise,
And a horse is bigger than me.
I'm smaller than a horse,
So, what is smaller than me?

A horse is heavier than a tortoise,
And a horse is heavier than me.
I'm lighter than a horse,
So what is lighter than me?

E **Learn Grammar** **Comparative Adjectives**

A ball is light**er than** a desk.

Is a desk heav**ier than** a ball? Yes, it is.

What's slow**er than** an airplane? A train is slow**er than** an airplane.

Look at the groups of things and compare them with your partner.

What's bigger than a car?

A bus is bigger than a car. Is a truck bigger than a bus?

F **Look around the room. Compare things with your partner.**

Is a book bigger than a chair?

Communicate

Words

A **Listen and point to the words. Listen again and say the words.** 3•13

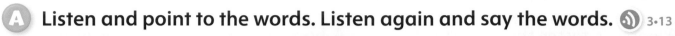

computer mouse

stapler

suitcase

broom

door

desk drawer

B **Write the words from A.**

1 We use this to keep the kitchen floor clean. broom

2 We put clothes in this when we go on vacation. ____________

3 We can use this to go online or write an e-mail. ____________

4 We push or pull this when we go in or go out. ____________

5 We put pencils, pens, notebooks, and papers in this. ____________

6 We can keep papers together with this. ____________

Listening

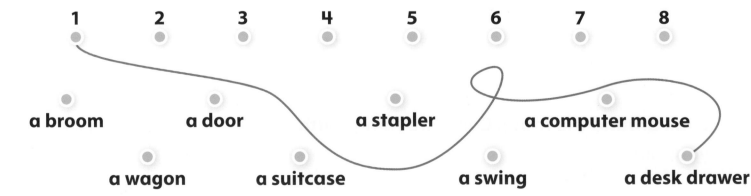

Think **What things do you push every day?**

C **Listen. How many of these things do you have?** 3•14

D **Listen again and match.** 3•15

1 2 3 4 5 6 7 8

a broom a door a stapler a computer mouse

a wagon a suitcase a swing a desk drawer

Speaking

E **Listen and repeat. Then practice with your partner. Use the words in the box to help.** 3•16

Help!
Oh, boy!
cool
awesome
You're welcome.
Don't mention it.

Word Study

F **Learn** Antonyms

Some words mean opposite things. These words are called **antonyms**.

heavy → light   **nervous** → calm

Write the antonym.

1 safe dangerous
2 happy ________
3 loud ________
4 interesting ________
5 polite ________
6 high ________

Write **Tell your partner about something you push and something you pull. Now write about them in your Workbook.** page 135

BIG QUESTION 8

What makes things move?

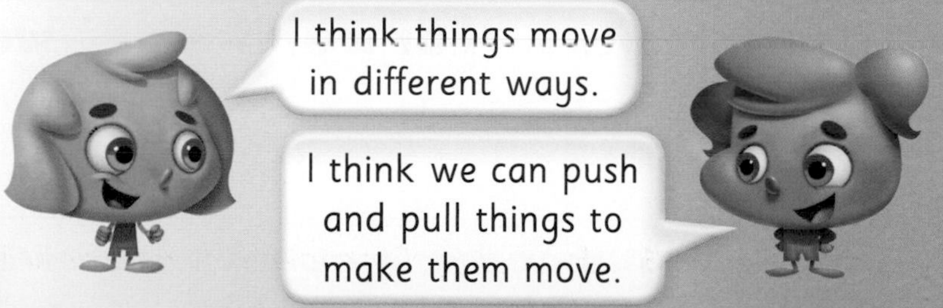

I think things move in different ways.
I think we can push and pull things to make them move.

UNIT 16 Get Ready

Words

A Listen and point to the words. Listen again and say the words. 3•17

stubborn

angry

goat

mountain

west east

forward

horns

wet

B Circle the one that does not belong.

1	feel:	angry	bird	stubborn
2	go up:	a hill	a mountain	a book
3	see:	a goat	a bird	stubborn
4	have:	west	a goat	horns
5	go:	backward	wet	forward
6	get:	wet	hot	mountain
7	travel:	ground	east	west
8	move:	forward	wet	fast

Before You Read

Think Are you sometimes stubborn? Is there a mountain near your town or city?

C **Learn** Theme

Remember, the theme of a story is the most important thing the writer wants you to understand. The writer is often teaching something important.

Read the story. Then circle the theme.

It's a cold and rainy day and Josh can't play outside. His mom sees his sad face and says, "Let's make some fun things." They make a toy car and Josh pushes and pulls the car on the table.

"This is fun," he says. Then they make a toy boat. Josh pushes his boat across the water in the kitchen sink.

"This is fun, too," he says. "Thanks for a great day, Mom."

a You can't play outside when it's rainy.
b It's good to play inside with your mom.
c It's good to think of things to do inside when it's rainy.

D **The story on pages 158–159 is about two stubborn goats who don't get along. What do you think they fight about? Give one idea.**

PREVIEW

Two Stubborn Little Goats

This story is a *fable*. A fable is a short story that teaches us a lesson.

Read 3·18

Two Stubborn Little Goats

A long time ago, a family of goats lived on East Mountain. Two of the brothers, Black Goat and Brown Goat, always fought about who was the best in the family. They were very stubborn: they never said "sorry" or "I'm wrong."

One day, they were on a small patch of the greenest grass on East Mountain. It was only enough for one goat. Brown Goat said, "I'm the oldest brother in the family, so I should eat the grass."

Black Goat said, "I'm the smartest brother in the family, so I should eat the grass."

They pushed each other with their horns. They pushed with the same force, so they didn't move forward or backward. They pushed for a long time and then they both got tired and fell down. Black Goat was angry so he moved to West Mountain.

There was a very narrow bridge between East Mountain and West Mountain. Every day Brown Goat crossed it to drink from the coldest water in the pond on West Mountain. Every day Black Goat crossed it to eat the juiciest grass on East Mountain. Brown Goat always crossed early, and Black Goat always crossed late.

One day, Brown Goat got up late so both goats were on the bridge at the same time. Brown Goat said, "Go back! I'm the oldest so I should cross first." Black Goat said, "You go back! I'm the smartest so I should cross first."

Think

What are the most important parts of the story so far?

They pushed each other with their horns. They pushed with the same force so they didn't move forward or backward.

They pushed for a long time and then they both got tired and fell into the river below the bridge.

The goats swam to the riverbank. Then they slowly walked home to their mountains. They were angry, tired, wet, cold, and hungry. And that's what happens to stubborn little goats.

Think

What are the most important parts of the story?

Understand

Comprehension

Think **What do you like about the story? Check (✓). Why? Give one reason.**

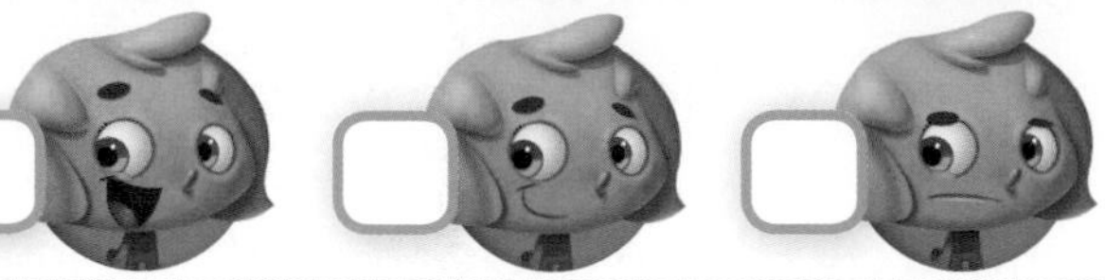

1 Black Goat and Brown Goat push each other. ☐ ☐ ☐

2 Black Goat moves to West Mountain. ☐ ☐ ☐

3 Black Goat and Brown Goat get wet. ☐ ☐ ☐

A Ask and answer the question.

What's your favorite part?

They fall into the river. It's funny!

B Circle the correct theme of the fable.

a Brothers shouldn't be kind to each other.

b People should share things.

c Being stubborn doesn't make us happy.

C Answer the questions.

1 Why didn't Black Goat and Brown Goat get along?

____

2 Why didn't the goats move when they pushed each other?

____

3 Did they like each other at the end of the story?

____

Think **What do you think?**

1 Why can it be bad to be stubborn? Give one reason.

2 Can you think of a good solution to Black Goat and Brown Goat's problem?

Workbook Grammar
pages 140–141

Grammar in Use

D Listen and sing along. **Two Brother Goats** 3•19

Two brother goats lived high in the mountains.
Whose voice was the best?
Each goat tried to shout the loudest,
Louder than all the rest.

"Yo da lay hee hoo, yo da lay hey hoo!"
Shouted one brother.
"Yo da lay hee hoo, yo da lay hey hoo!"
Shouted the other.

"You're the quietest goat! I'm the loudest goat!"
Shouted one brother.
"I'm the loudest goat! You're the quietest goat!"
Shouted the other.

E **Learn Grammar** Superlative Adjectives

I'm the young**est** person in my family.
Is the juic**iest** grass on East Mountain? Yes, it is.

Look at the pictures. Ask questions with your partner.

Is the man the oldest person?
Yes, he is.

F Talk about your family with your partner.

My father is the biggest person in my family.

Communicate

Words

A Listen and point to the words. Listen again and say the words. 3•20

basketball

soccer

tennis

baseball

hockey

golf

B Think about the words in **A** and add them to the chart.

Played with a team		Not played with a team
1 basketball	3	1
2	4	2

Listening

Think What's your favorite sport?

C Listen. Which sport doesn't use a ball? 3•21

D Listen again and write. 3•22

They're playing ...

1 ______ 4 ______

2 ______ 5 ______

3 ______ 6 ______

Speaking

E Tell your partner about a sport you like. Act it out. Your partner guesses the sport. Use the words in boxes to help. 3•23

I run, jump, and throw the ball.
You're playing basketball.
I kick ...
I throw ...
You like ...

Writing Study

F **Learn** Comparative and Superlative Endings

When a word has one syllable, we add -er or -est.

small → smaller → smallest

When a word has more than one syllable and ends in a "y", we drop the "y" and add -ier or -iest.

heavy → heavier → heaviest

Write the comparative and superlative.

1 fast	faster ______	______	
2 funny	______	______	
3 lonely	______	______	
4 clean	______	______	
5 hungry	______	______	
6 healthy	______	______	

Write Tell your partner about the speed and movement in a sport you like to play. Now write about it in your **Workbook**. page 143

Wrap Up

A **Listen and read along.** 3•24

Dot and her family were excited about their vacation.
Vacation time! We went to the mountains in the east.
Where's Gus?
My suitcase is the heaviest.
We played hockey with brooms on the frozen pond. But we couldn't find Gus!
This is fun!
I'm all wet!
But where's Gus?
We played basketball on the hard ground. We threw the ball to each other.
Don't be stubborn.
It's my turn!
Then we wanted to play soccer.
Where's the soccer ball?
Look in the suitcase.
We found the ball – and we found Gus! It was the best vacation ever.
Go forward!
I'm faster than all of you.

Project: Make a Forces Poster

B **Make a forces poster.**

- Write sentences about things that are easy and hard to push and pull.
- Find or draw pictures.

My Forces Poster
Easy to Push and Pull
Hard to Push and Pull
The hat is easy to pull on my head.
The wagon is hard to pull.
The doorbell is easy to push.
The department store door is hard to push.
My suitcase is easy to pull.
The trash can is hard to pull.

C **Put your forces poster on the wall. Tell the class about your poster.**

The hat is easy to pull onto my head. The wagon is hard to pull.

D **Walk around the room. Look at the posters. Act out one of the actions on a poster. Your partner guesses.**

BIG QUESTION 8

What makes things move?

A **Watch the video.**

B **Think more about the Big Question.**

C **Complete the Big Question Chart.**

What did you learn about how things move?

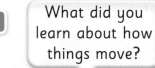

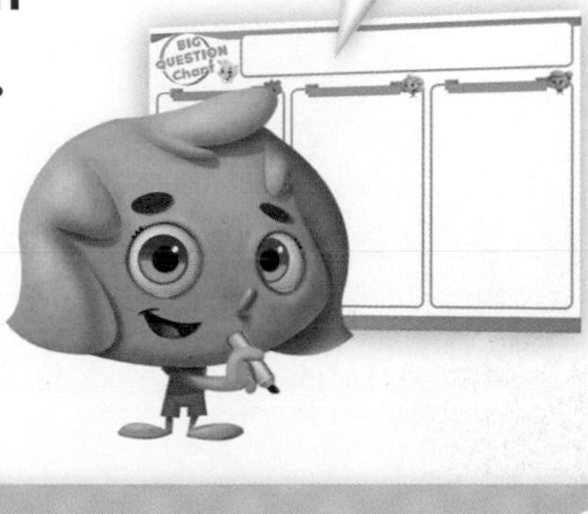

In units **17** and **18** you will:

WATCH a video about art.

LEARN about where we see shapes in our world.

READ about a girl who makes origami.

WRITE about shapes you use in art.

MAKE an art report.

BIG QUESTION 9

How do we make art?

A Watch the video.

B Look at the picture. What do you see?

1 What are the children doing?

2 What are they using to make art?

C Think and answer the questions.

1 What do you like to draw?

2 Where can you see art?

D Fill out the **Big Question Chart**.

What do you know about art?
BIG QUESTION Chart

UNIT 17 Get Ready

Words

A Listen and point to the words. Listen again and say the words. 3•25

crescent

star

spiral

oval

straight

nature

collage

sculpture

pattern

B Circle the correct word.

1 nature / spiral

2 round / oval

3 straight / star

4 plain / pattern

5 collage / sculpture

6 crescent / round

7 spiral / straight

8 painting / sculpture

9 star / round

Before You Read

Think What shapes can you see in your classroom?
What are your favorite shapes to draw?

C **Learn** Text-to-Self Connection

When we read something, we can think about things in our lives that are similar to things in the text.

The story of two stubborn goats.
I am stubborn, too.

The text about rules.
My mom makes the rules at home.

Read the text. Think.

There's an interesting art park in New York. It only has sculptures. In good weather a lot of people come to the park. They enjoy the art and sometimes they have picnics.

1 *There's an interesting art park in New York.* Think about what's in your city.
2 *In good weather a lot of people come to the park.* Think about what you do in good weather.
3 *People enjoy the art.* Think about what you enjoy.

D **The text on pages 170–171 is about shapes. What shapes do you think are in the text? Think of five shapes.**

PREVIEW

Shapes In Art

In this text we learn about shapes in art.

This text is an *informational text*. Remember, informational texts tell us about our world.

Art

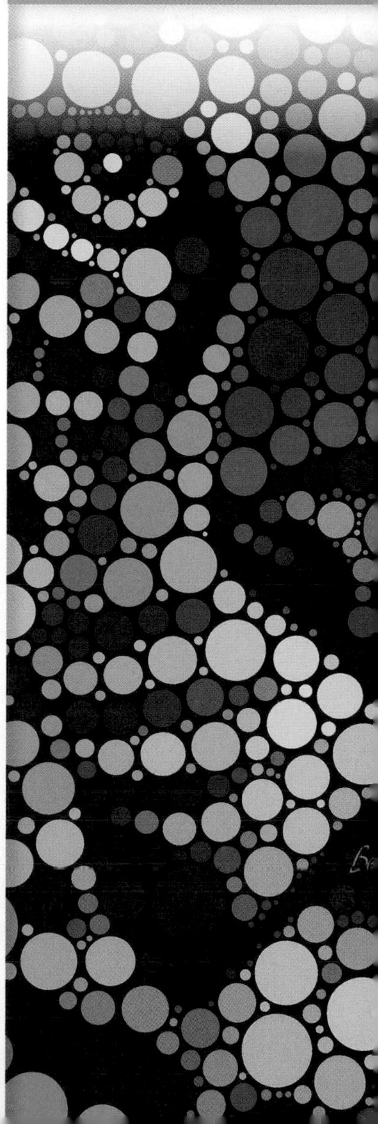

Read 3•26

Shapes In Art

We can see shapes in people, animals, nature, art, and much more in our world. They are all around us.

Kinds of Shapes

Squares and rectangles have four straight sides and four corners. How are squares and rectangles different?

A square has four corners and all four sides are the same length.

A rectangle also has four corners but two sides are longer than the other two.

Circles and ovals don't have straight lines or corners. How are circles and ovals different?

All triangles have three straight lines and three corners.

Stars, crescents, and spirals are all very different kinds of shapes.

Stars have lots of sides.

Crescents have two sides, but they aren't straight.

Spirals don't have sides and they don't have straight lines or corners.

What shapes do you see in this nature collage?

Think

Think about things in nature that you see every day. What shapes are they?

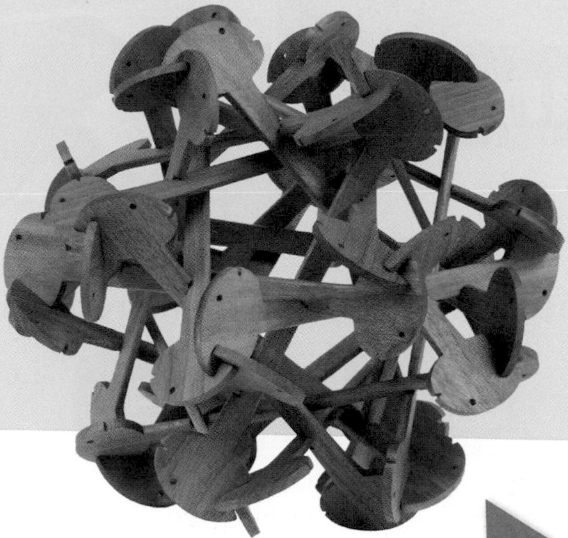

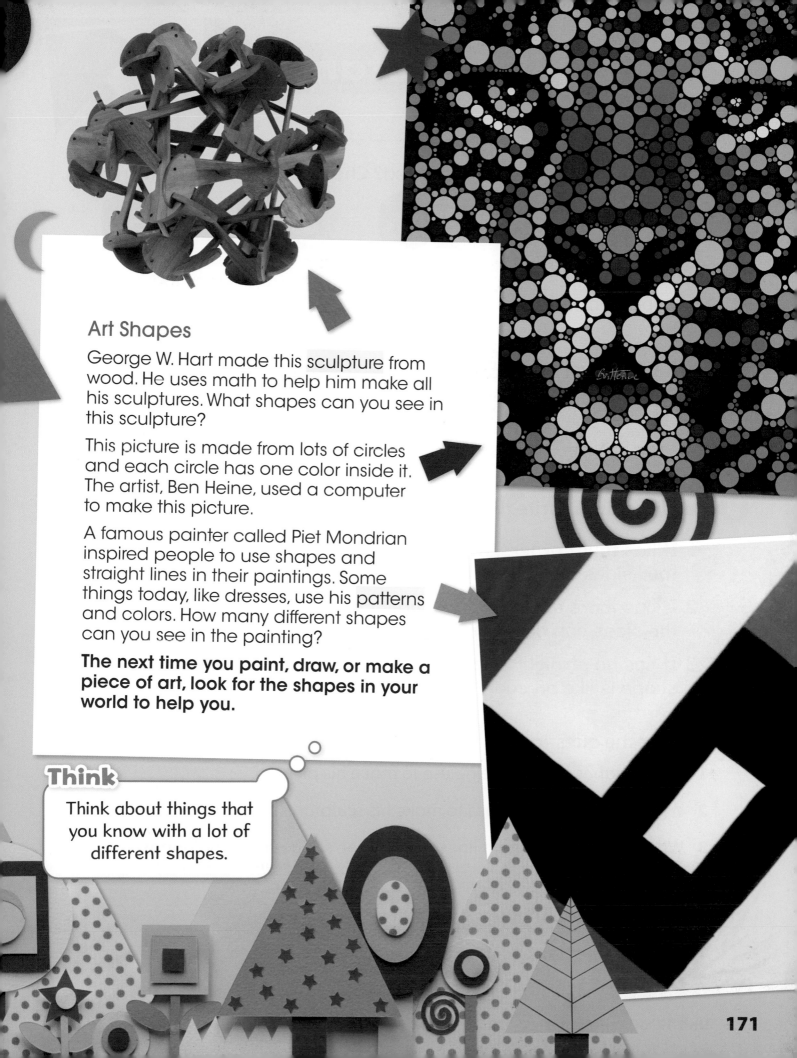

Art Shapes

George W. Hart made this sculpture from wood. He uses math to help him make all his sculptures. What shapes can you see in this sculpture?

This picture is made from lots of circles and each circle has one color inside it. The artist, Ben Heine, used a computer to make this picture.

A famous painter called Piet Mondrian inspired people to use shapes and straight lines in their paintings. Some things today, like dresses, use his patterns and colors. How many different shapes can you see in the painting?

The next time you paint, draw, or make a piece of art, look for the shapes in your world to help you.

Think

Think about things that you know with a lot of different shapes.

Understand

Comprehension

Think What do you like about the text? Check (✓). Why? Give one reason.

1 Different shapes	☐	☐	☐
2 Shapes in nature	☐	☐	☐
3 Shapes in art	☐	☐	☐

A Ask and answer the question.

What's your favorite part?
The leopard picture with circles. It's cool!

B Read the clues. Write the shapes.

1 It has four corners, four straight sides, and all four sides are the same length.	square
2 It has three straight sides, three corners, and the sides can be different lengths.	
3 It has no straight sides, no corners, and the shape is like an egg.	

C Answer the questions.

1 What shapes did Ben Heine use to make his picture? ______

2 What did George Hart use to make his sculptures? ______

3 What artist uses straight lines to make the shapes in his paintings?

______

Think What do you think?

1 Were George Hart's sculptures easy to make?

2 Can we see shapes in all paintings?

Grammar in Use

D Listen and sing along. **Triangles** 3•27

Your collage has green triangles,
And yellow, orange, and blue.
It has a pattern like a star,
And it has some stickers too.

There is a lot of pasta,
And a lot of paper there.
But there aren't any spirals,
Not a crescent, not a square.

The triangles in your art work
Are big and tall and small.
But don't look for any ovals,
That shape isn't there at all!

E **Learn Grammar** Quantifiers

Things we can count	Things we can't count
There are a lot of shapes.	There is a lot of paper.
There aren't any triangles.	There isn't any red paint.

Look at the shape collages. What can you count? What can't you count?

F Look again at the shape collages. Practice with your partner.

There's a lot of snow in this collage.

But there aren't any flowers.

Communicate

Words

A Listen and point to the words. Listen again and say the words. 3•28

photograph

origami

drawing

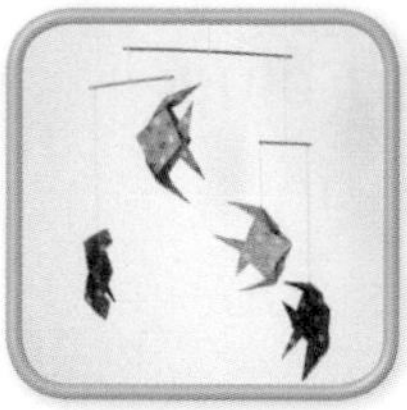
mobile

oil painting

mosaic

B Look at the things we use to make art. What kind of art is it?

1 mosaic

2 ______

3 ______

4 ______

5 ______

6 ______

Listening

Think What do you like better, paintings or photographs? Why?

C Listen. Where is the boy taking photographs? 3•29

D Listen again and circle the correct answer. 3•30

They're talking about ...

1 a collage / (a photograph) / a drawing
2 a mosaic / a mobile / origami
3 a sculpture / a mosaic / an oil painting
4 a drawing / a photograph / an oil painting
5 a mobile / an oil painting / a mosaic
6 a drawing / a mobile / a sculpture

Speaking

E **Listen and repeat. Then practice with a partner. Use the words in the box to help.** 3•31

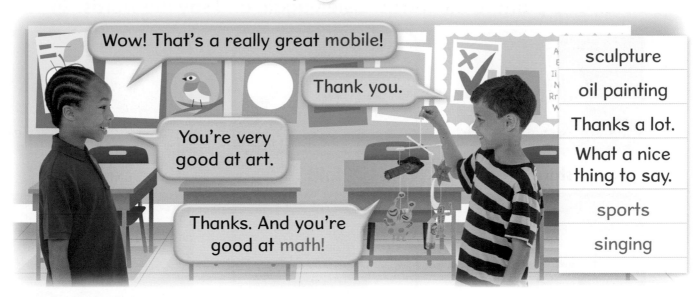

sculpture
oil painting
Thanks a lot.
What a nice thing to say.
sports
singing

Word Study

F **Learn** Homophones

Some words sound the same but aren't spelled the same.
These words are called **homophones**. **flower** → **flour**

Write the homophones.

won	ate	rode
be	too	write

1 right ______ 4 road ______

2 one ______ 5 two ______

3 eight ______ 6 bee ______

Write **Tell your partner about your favorite kind of art and the shapes you use. Now write about it in your Workbook.** page 153

BIG QUESTION 9

How do we make art?

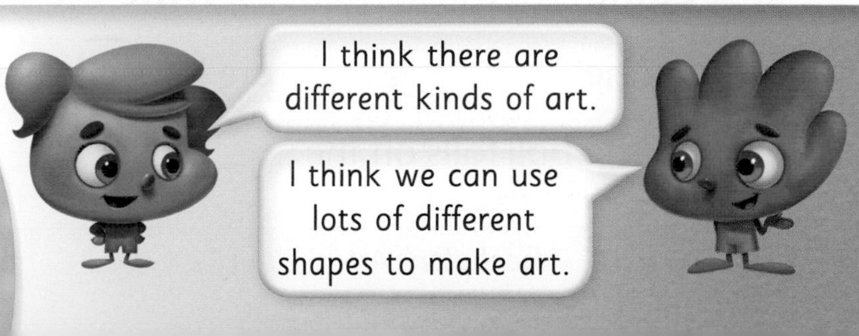

I think there are different kinds of art.
I think we can use lots of different shapes to make art.

UNIT 18 Get Ready

Words

A Listen and point to the words. Listen again and say the words. 3•32

shiny

fold

edge

crane

seal

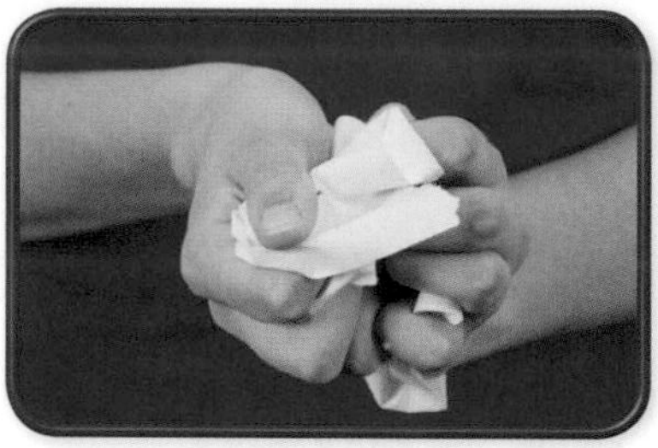

crumple

waves

climb

golden

B Look at **A** and write the words.

1 Animals: crane ____________

2 Things we can do: ____________ ____________ ____________

3 How things look: ____________ ____________

C Complete the sentences. Write the words from **A**.

1 The ____________ are big in the sea today.

2 The ball falls off the ____________ of the table.

Before You Read

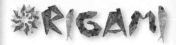

Think Do you ever draw pictures for the stories you write? What do you like to draw?

D **Learn** Text-to-Self Connection

Remember, when we read something, we should think about things in our lives that are similar to things in the text.

Read the text. Then write sentences.

Finn loves art. He goes to art class on Thursdays. Finn likes music, too, and he's good at it. One day in art class, he made a musical instrument collage. It was beautiful. He took the bus home.

"Where's your collage?" asked his mom.

"Oh, no!" he said. "I left it on the bus." He was really sad.

1 Think about what **you** like.

____

2 Think about what **you're** good at.

____

3 Think about things **you** forgot.

____

E **In the story a girl makes a lot of paper animals. What kinds of animals do you think she makes?**

PREVIEW

ORIGAMI

In this story we read about a little girl who likes to make things.

This story is a *panel story*. A panel story has a lot of scenes. Each scene has a picture and some words.

Susannah Appelbaum is the author of the famous *Poisons of Caux* series for young readers. She loves using her imagination to create fun, new worlds.

Read 3•33

ORIGAMI

Maki woke up early. Her room was quiet. Everyone was sleeping, even her little sister Akiko in the bed next to hers.

What could she do? *I know,* she thought. *I can do orgami!* On the table was some colored paper.

Maki got out of bed quietly. The paper was shiny, and there were a lot of colors.

Maki folded a red square, bending the paper in the middle and at the edges. She worked until it was done. Suddenly, it was a crane!

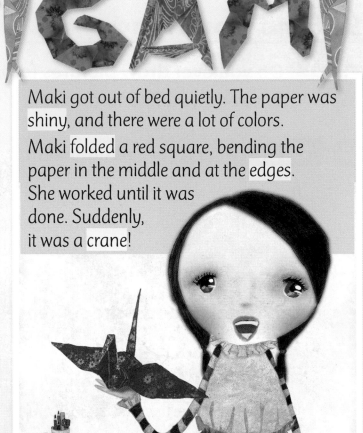

The crane looked lonely, so she made another—this time a blue one. Soon she had a whole row of origami cranes!

"Would you like some friends?" Maki asked the cranes.

"Oh, yes!" said the cranes.

"You can speak?" Maki laughed.

"Of course. You're in our origami world now!" So Maki picked up more paper.

Think

Think about animals that you like.

She made an orange seal. Seals like to play, Maki knew, so she made him a purple ball.

"Thanks," said the seal. And he rolled the ball back to her. They played and played until Maki had another idea.

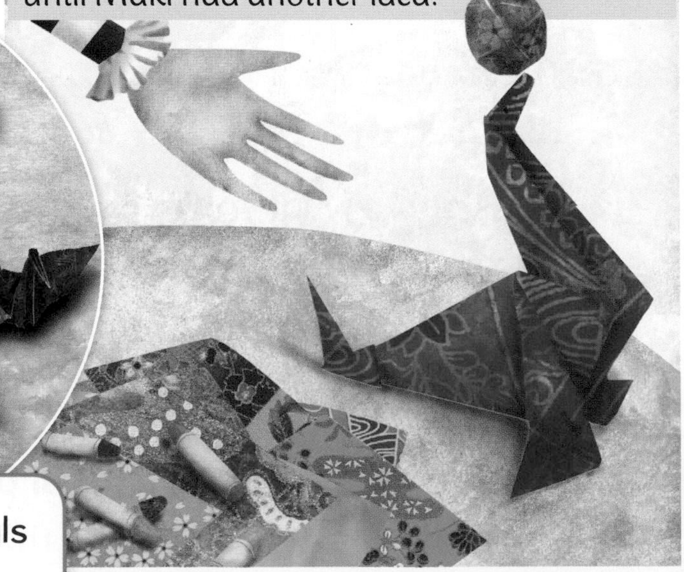

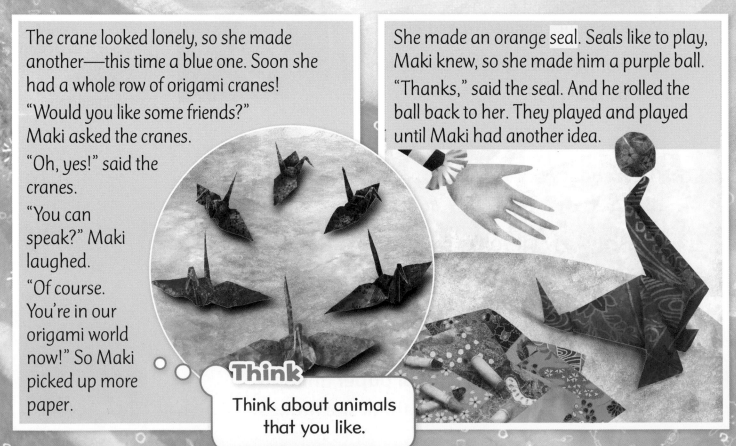

With blue paper, Maki made water, crumpling it to make waves. Maki dived into the water and swam happily with the cranes and seal. A green fish jumped through the air.

But something was missing. Maki remembered her sister, Akiko. She missed her and wanted to see her.

Think

Think about things you like to make.

Maki saw a sailboat. The boat came near, and Maki heard a voice.

"All aboard!" the voice said.

Maki looked up. It was her sister's voice! Akiko was awake and looking for her in the origami world.

Think

Think about things that you like to do.

She climbed into the sailboat. "Hello, Akiko!," she said. Her new friends looked at her from the water, smiling.

In Maki's hands was one last piece of paper. It was golden. Maki folded it, threw it high into the air, and made a big, round sun.

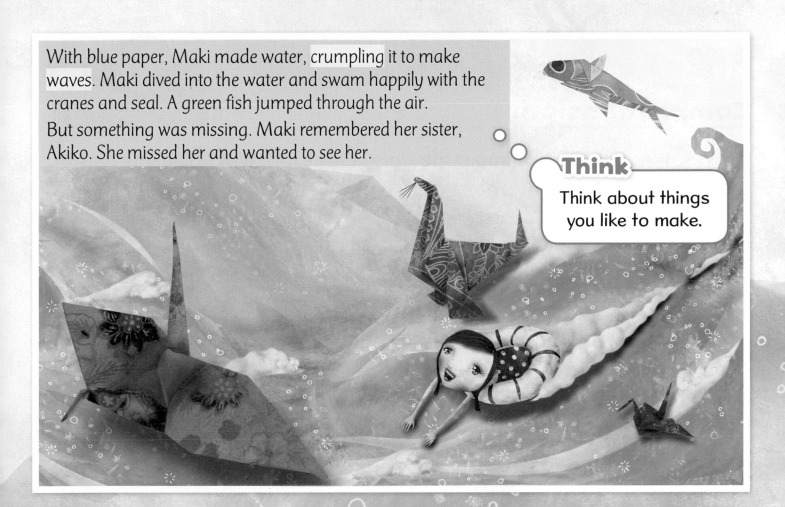

Understand

Comprehension

Think **What do you like about the story? Check (✓). Why? Give one reason.**

1 Maki makes origami cranes and a seal.	☐	☐	☐
2 Maki plays in the water with the animals.	☐	☐	☐
3 Maki misses her sister.	☐	☐	☐
4 Maki makes a golden sun.	☐	☐	☐

A Ask and answer the question.

What's your favorite part?

Maki makes an orange seal. That's my favorite color!

B Number the events in the correct order.

☐ Maki makes origami animals.

☐ Maki makes a golden sun.

☐ Maki plays in the sea.

1 Maki wakes up.

☐ Maki enters the origami world.

☐ Maki sees a boat.

C Answer the questions.

1 When Maki woke up what did she see? ______________________

2 What animals did she make? ______________________

3 Why did Maki get onto the sailboat? ______________________

Think **What do you think?**

1 Did Maki really have this adventure?

2 Do we need a lot of toys to have fun?

Workbook Grammar
pages 158–159

Grammar in Use

D Listen and sing along. **Let's Paint Together** 3•34

Do you have any green paint?
No, but I have some blue.
How much blue paint do you have?
A lot - here's some for you.
Let's paint together - art is fun to do!

Do you have any paper?
Yes, and paintbrushes, too.
How many paintbrushes do you have?
A few - here's one for you.
Let's paint together - art is fun to do!

E **Learn Grammar** Quantifiers

Did Maki have any pencils? No, she didn't.
How many seals were there? There was one seal.
How much paper was there? There was a lot of paper.

How much is there? How many are there? Practice with your partner.

How much snow is there in the drawing?
There's a lot of snow.

F Look around the classroom. Ask your partner about the things you can see.

Communicate

Words

A Listen and point to the words. Listen again and say the words. 3•35

markers

scissors

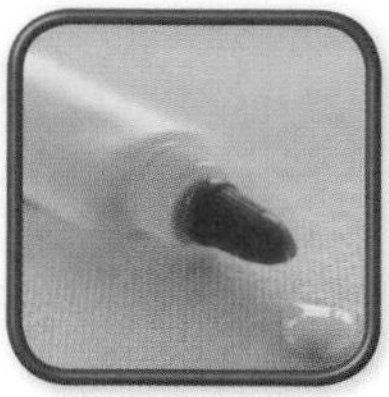
glue

watercolors

chalk

colored pencils

B Think about the words in **A** and add them to the chart.

Use to draw		Don't use to draw
1 markers	3	1
2	4	2

Listening

Think What art do you make at home?

C Listen. What does Grant make? 3•36

D Listen again and check the things they use or need. Then circle. 3•37

1

a mosaic
b collage

2

a mobile
b sculpture

3
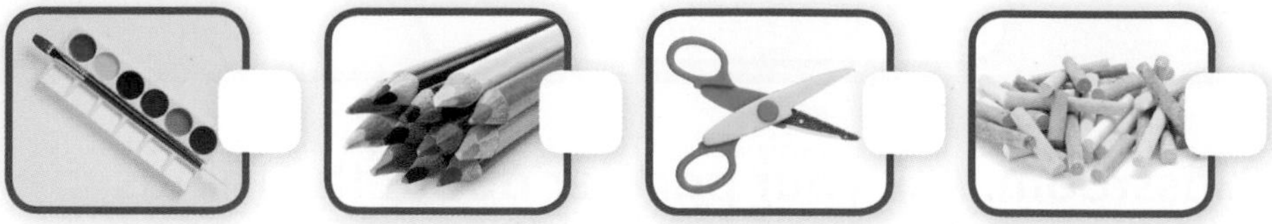

a origami
b mosaic

Speaking

E **Describe a piece of art. Ask a partner to guess what kind of art it is. Use the words in boxes to help.** 3•38

It's a picture of the rainforest. I used green and brown pieces of stone for the trees.
You made a mosaic.
Aa Bb Cc Dd
Ee Ff Gg Hh
Ii Jj Kk Ll Mm
Nn Oo Pp Qq
I used ...
It has ...
You made ...

Writing Study

F **Learn** Using Commas in Lists

We use **commas** in a sentence to separate three or more items in a list.

My sister bought glue, a box of markers, colored pencils, scissors, and chalk.

Write commas in the sentences below.

1 You can take a bus a train or an airplane.

2 My sister made ice cream with cream salt sugar and peaches.

3 The students were hungry thirsty and tired.

4 My friend is friendly polite and thoughtful.

Write **Talk about the art tools you usually use in your art projects. Now write about them in your Workbook.** page 161

Wrap Up

A **Listen and read along.** 3•39

The children are at their Art Club.
Dot, please show the class what you made.
Dot made an animal mobile.
I painted some straight lines for the long legs of my crane.
Layla made a sculpture of the sky at night.
I like shapes. I made a crescent and a lot of stars.
Billy made a drawing of a golden horse in the sunlight.
How many ovals and circles can you see in my drawing?
Zak made an origami boat.
I folded the paper to make the boat, and I crumpled paper to make the sea.
Gus made an oil painting.
Uh, that's very interesting, Gus. But what is it?
It's me!

Project: Make an Art Report

B **Make an art report.**

- Choose a favorite piece of art and write about it.
- Bring or draw a picture of it to show the class.

The Starry Night Report

I like this painting very much. It's called The Starry Night. It's an oil painting. Vincent Van Gogh painted it in 1889. I like the shapes in the painting. The stars are circles, the moon is a crescent and the clouds are spirals. I think the colors are beautiful, too.

C **Put your art report on the wall. Tell the class about the piece of art.**

I like this painting because of all the different shapes and colors.

D **Walk around the room. Look at all the reports. Find one you like. Tell your partner.**

I like the mosaic in Maria's report. The shapes are very interesting.

BIG QUESTION 9

How do we make art?

A **Watch the video.** ▶

B **Think more about the Big Question.**

C **Complete the Big Question Chart.**

Bandar, the Greedy Monkey

Characters (19 + total): *Bandar (the monkey), Baker, Candy maker, Gardener, Cook, Narrators x10 (holding signs), Chorus 3+*
Props: *signs for The Town, Bakery, Garden, Restaurant, Candy Store*

Bandar *sits by the tree on the left of the stage. The* ***Narrator*** *enters holding the* ***Town sign*** *and stands on the right of the stage.*

Narrator: This is a play about Bandar, a very greedy, little monkey. Bandar lives in the woods near a small town.

Bandar: I'm very bored and I'm very hungry. What can I do?

Bandar *looks around and sees the town.*

Aha! I have a good idea.

Bandar *runs to the* ***Town sign****, then walks around the stage.*

Narrator: Bandar goes to the town. He walks around the town and sees a bakery.

The ***Narrator*** *holds up the* ***Bakery sign*** *and the* ***Baker*** *holding a plate of cookies enters.*

Bandar: Cookies, cookies, I can see.
Cookies, cookies, more than three.
Cookies, cookies all for me.

Bandar *grabs some cookies, then runs away, eating cookies as he runs.*

Chorus: Bandar is greedy as can be. He stole fifteen cookies as you can see.

The ***Baker*** *chases* ***Bandar****.*

Baker: You greedy, little monkey. I had thirty cookies. How many do I have left?'

Narrator: You have fifteen cookies left.

The ***Narrator*** *holds up the* ***Garden sign*** *and the* ***Gardener*** *enters. The* ***Gardener*** *digs up some carrots in the garden.*

Bandar: Carrots, carrots, I can see.
Carrots, carrots, more than three.
Carrots, carrots all for me.

Bandar *grabs some carrots, then runs away, eating carrots as he runs.*

Chorus: Bandar is greedy as can be. He stole sixteen carrots as you can see.

The ***Gardener*** *looks at his carrot patch, then chases* ***Bandar****.*

Gardener: You greedy, little monkey. I had sixty carrots. How many do I have left?

Narrator: You have forty-four carrots left.

The ***Narrator*** *holds up the* ***Restaurant sign*** *and the* ***Cook*** *holding a plate of sausages enters.*

Bandar: Sausages, sausages, I can see.
Sausages, sausages, more than three.
Sausages, sausages all for me.

***Bandar** grabs some sausages, then runs away, eating sausages as he runs.*

Chorus: Bandar is greedy as can be. He stole twelve sausages as you can see.

*The **Cook** chases **Bandar**.*

Cook: You greedy, little monkey. I had forty-two sausages. How many do I have left?

Narrator: You have thirty sausages left.

*The **Baker**, **Gardener**, and **Cook** enter and chase **Bandar**. Then they all leave the stage.*

Narrator: The baker, the gardener, and the cook are angry. They chase Bandar all over town.

*The **Narrator** holds up the **Candy Store sign** and the **Candy maker** enters.*

Candy maker: How can we catch greedy little Bandar?

Narrator: The candy maker has a very good idea!

*The **Candy maker** puts two jars on the stage and leaves. **Bandar** enters.*

Bandar: Candies, candies, I can see.
Candies, candies, more than three.
Candies, candies all for me.

***Bandar** puts his hands in the jars and grabs as much candy as he can. The **Candy maker** enters.*

Candy maker: You greedy little monkey! Let go of the candies and you can run away!

***Bandar** tries to get his hands full of candy out of the jars.*

Bandar: No! No! I want the candies.

Candy maker: Silly, greedy monkey! I can catch you now!

Chorus: Bandar is greedy as can be. He doesn't let go as you can see.

Narrator: The candy maker catches Bandar.

Candy maker: Back to the woods you go. And NEVER come back to town again, you silly, greedy little monkey.

*The **Candy maker** and **Bandar** leave the stage.*

Narrator: And Bandar the greedy monkey never went to that town again.

***Everyone** enters.*

Narrator: The lesson of this story is …

Everyone: It's not good to be greedy. It's not good to steal.

Two Stubborn Little Goats

Characters (21 total): *Mother Goat, Father Goat, White Goat, Black Goat, Brown Goat,* ***Narrators:*** *Up to 16*
Props: *cardboard goat masks, cardboard cutout for small patch of grass, cardboard cutout bridge, (cardboard cutout river), cardboard cutout for a pond, signs for East Mountain and West Mountain*

***Mother**, **Father**, and **White Goat** enter from the right. **Brown Goat** and **Black Goat** enter from the left.*

Narrator: A long time ago, a goat family lived on East Mountain. Two of the brothers, Black Goat and Brown Goat, always fought about who was the best in the family.

Narrator: They were very stubborn and they never said "sorry" or "I'm wrong."

Chorus: Two very stubborn goats.
They fight all day long.
Black Goat's always right.
Brown Goat's never wrong.

***Adult goats** and **White Goat** move to the far right of the stage. **Brown Goat** and **Black Goat** move to the grass patch.*

Narrator: One day, they were at a small patch of the greenest grass on East Mountain.

Narrator: Only one goat could eat at a time.

Brown Goat: I'm the oldest brother in the family so I should eat the grass!

Black Goat: I'm the smartest brother in the family so I should eat the grass!

***Brown Goat** and **Black Goat** push each other with their horns. They don't move.*

Narrator: They pushed each other with their horns. They pushed with the same force so they didn't move forward or backward.

Narrator: They pushed for a long time and then they both got tired and fell down.

***Black Goat** and **Brown Goat** fall down.*

Chorus: They pushed each other with their horns.
They pushed all day long.
Black Goat's always right.
Brown Goat's never wrong.

***Black Goat** gets up and crosses the bridge. He looks angrily at **Brown Goat**.*

Narrator: Black Goat was angry so he moved to West Mountain.

Narrator: There was a very narrow bridge between East and West Mountain.

***Brown Goat** crosses the bridge, drinks from the pond, then returns.*

Narrator: Every day Brown Goat crossed the bridge to drink from the coldest water in the pond on West Mountain.

***Black Goat** crosses the bridge, eats from the grass, then returns.*

Narrator: Every day Black Goat crossed the bridge to eat the juiciest grass on East Mountain.

Narrator: Brown Goat always crossed early and Black Goat always crossed late.

***Brown Goat** and **Black Goat** both cross the bridge at the same time and meet each other in the middle.*

Narrator: One day both goats were on the bridge at the same time. It was too narrow for both goats to cross.

Brown Goat: Go back! I'm the oldest so I should cross first.

Black Goat: You go back! I'm the smartest so I should cross first.

***Brown Goat** and **Black Goat** lock horns and push each other. They don't move.*

Narrator: They pushed each other with their horns. They pushed with the same force so they didn't move forward or backward.

***Black Goat** and **Brown Goat** both fall off the bridge and into the river.*

Narrator: They pushed for a long time. They both got tired and fell into the river below the bridge.

***Black Goat** and **Brown Goat** swim to opposite riverbanks. They start walking slowly in opposite directions, looking very angry.*

Narrator: The goats swam to the riverbank. Then they slowly walked home to their mountains. They were angry, tired, wet, cold and hungry.

Adult Goats and White Goat Chorus:

They pushed each other with their horns
And fell into the river.
Cold, wet and very tired
Look at the brothers shiver!

***Brown Goat** and **Black Goat** leave the stage.*

Narrator: They went home. And that is what happens to stubborn little goats.

***Everyone** enters.*

Chorus: Don't be stubborn like the goats
If you want to get along.
Don't think you're always right
And you're never ever wrong!

World Map

Ricky Racoon
Page 98
Let's Make Ice Cream!
Page 38
A Juice Carton's Diary
Page 118
Olga's Flute
Page 138
Don't Be Grabby, Gorilla
Page 98

Two Stubborn Little Goats
Page 158
Tell Me a Story, Grandpa
Page 58
Origami
Page 178
Bears Always Share
Page 99
Bandar, the Greedy Monkey
Page 78
Then and Now
Page 50
The Ox Always Knocks
Page 99
Leo and Lily's Adventure
Page 18

OXFORD
UNIVERSITY PRESS

Great Clarendon Street, Oxford, OX2 6DP, United Kingdom

Oxford University Press is a department of the University of Oxford. It furthers the University's objective of excellence in research, scholarship, and education by publishing worldwide. Oxford is a registered trade mark of Oxford University Press in the UK and in certain other countries

First published in 2014
2019
11

ISBN: 978 0 19 427863 8

Printed in China

This book is printed on paper from certified and well-managed sources

ACKNOWLEDGEMENTS

The authors and publisher are grateful to those who have given permission to reproduce the following extracts and adaptations of copyright material:

"Bears Always Share", "Don't Be Grabby, Gorilla", "The Ox Always Knocks", "Welcome, Ricky Raccoon!", from THE PLEASE AND THANK YOU BOOK by Barbara Shook Hazan, text copyright © 1974 by Random House, Inc. Used by permission of Golden Books, an imprint of Random House Children's Book, a division of Random House, Inc. Any third party use of this material, outside of this publication, is prohibited. Interested parties must apply directly to Random House, Inc. for permission.

Oxford University Press would like to thank all of the teachers whose opinions helped to inform this series, and in particular, the following reviewers:

Egypt Samar Magdy Abdelfatah, Pioneers Language School; Sohair Saad, Orman Academy; **Korea** Seon-young Heo, Junggye Wonderland; Pan-Seob (Sean) Kim, Sean English Academy; So Young Kim; Yoo-Mi Suh, YM English School; **Mexico** Ana Cristina Alaluf Hernández, Colegio Teresiano, Mérida; Esperanza Medina Cruz, Centro Universitario Francisco Larroyo; Gabriela Martínez, Escuela Tomas Alva Edison Primaria; Laura Catalina Guevara Medina, Instituto Edinburgh; Pedro Olmos Medina, Colegio Carlos Chavez; **Oman** Jane Moates, English Language Consultant; **Turkey** Duygu Kiliç, Doğa Schools; Ozlem Şeftalioğlu, Bursa Final Schools; Sibel Ulukoy, ITU Foundation Schools, Dr. Natuk Birkan Primary School; **UAE** Sandra Qazamel, Al Ma'arifa International School

Illustrated characters Billy, Dot, Gus and Layla, the Songs and the Wrap Up stories all by: Luispa Salmon/ Lemonade Illustration Agency

Illustrations by: Wouter Bruneel/Andrea Brown Literary Agency, Inc. pp.57 (Tell Me a Story, Grandpa), 58, 59, 60 (boy and Grandpa); Design pp.10-11(Amazing Animals text, photos where used credited separately), 50-51 (tablet, newspaper, ticket, background icons), 70-71 (food items), 72 (cookies), 90-91 (illustrations and textures), 151 (tablet), 170-171 (cutting mat background); Christiane Engle/ Good Illustration Ltd pp.25 (rabbit), 45 (My Mixture Book), 65 (My Interview), 105 (My Rules Poster), 125 (My Tree Collage), 165 (My Forces Poster), 181 (Ex E beach, mobile, winter scene), 185 (The Starry Night Report); Finger Industries pp.69 (boy in glasses), 70-71 children; Guy Francis/Shannon Associates L.L.C pp.117 (A Juice Carton's Diary), 118, 119, 120 (juice carton); Sharon Harmer p.173 (Ex E shapes collages); John Haslam p.131; Cosei Kawa/Advocate-Art pp.177 (Origami), 178, 179, 180 (Maki); Dusan Lakicevic/Beehive Illustration pp.9, 17 (Ex D), 29 (Ex C), 37 (Ex D), 57 (Ex C), 69 (Ex C), 77 (Ex D), 89, 97 (Ex C), 109 (Ex C), 117 (Ex C), 129, 137 (Ex C), 149 (Ex C), 157 (Ex C), 169, 177 (Ex D); Marina Le Ray/ Advocate-Art pp.77 (Bandar, the Greedy Monkey), 78, 79, 80 (Bandar, Ex B), 186; Helen Musselwhite pp.170-171 (illustration and shapes); Garry Parsons pp.17 (Leo and Lily's Adventure), 18, 19, 20 (Leo and Lily), 149 (train, car, horse), 151, 152 (train, car, horse, boy); Marcin Piwowarski/The Bright Agency pp.37 (Let's Make Ice Cream!), 38, 39, 40 (Let's Make Ice Cream!); Mark Ruffle pp.29 (polar bear and seals), 30-31; Jamie Smith/MB Artists pp.16, 22, 33 (Ex E), 35 (Ex F), 41 (Ex E), 53 (Ex E), 61 (Ex E), 73 (Ex E), 81 (Ex E), 102 (Ex D), 113 (Ex E), 121 (Ex E), 133 (Ex E), 135 (Ex G), 141 (Ex E), 153 (Ex E), 156, 161 (Ex E), 176, 181 (Ex E desk and paper); Susan Swan pp.109 (frees and flowers), 110-111 (illustration and title), 112 (rubbish truck and chimneys); Mike Terry/The Bright Agency pp.97 (The Please and Thank You Book Poems), 98, 99, 100 (bears); Scott Wakefield/Shannon Associates L.L.C pp.157 (Two Stubborn Little Goats), 158, 159, 160 (two goats), 188; Laura Wood/Good Illustration Ltd pp.137 (Olga's Flute), 138, 139, 140 (Olga).

Commissioned photography by: Graham Alder at MM Studios with illustrated backgrounds by Mark Ruffle: pp.12 (headshots), 13 (headshots) 15 (park scene), 20, 23, 25, 32 (headshots), 33 (BL headshot and BR headshot), 35 (kitchenscene), 40, 41, 43, 45, 52 (headshots), 53, 55, 60, 61, 63, 65, 72, 73, 75, 80, 81, 83 (classroom scene), 85, 92 (headshots), 93, 95, 100, 101, 103, 105, 112 (headshots), 113, 115, 120, 121, 113, 115, 120, 121, 113, 115, 120, 121, 123, 125, 132 (headshots), 135, 140, 143, 145, 152, 155, 160, 161 (BL headshot and BR headshot), 163, 165, 172 (headshots), 175, 180, 181 (BL headshot and BR headshot), 183 and 185.

Props maker: Charlotte Stevens pp.23, 85, 155 (passport) and 145.

The Publishers would like to thank the following for their kind permission to reproduce photographs and other copyright material: Alamy pp.8 (feathers/Avalon), 8 (scales/Zoonar GmbH), 8 (frog/Derek Croucher), 10 (fish/Stocktrek Images, Inc.), 10 (eagle/T.Walker/Photri Images), 11 (frog/Photoshot Holdings Ltd), 12 (fish/Stocktrek Images, Inc.), 13 (feathers/VICTOR FRAILE), 13 (wing/imagebroker), 13 (hair/Hangon Media Works Private limited), 14 (starfish/dbimages), 14 (head/PetStockBoys), 14 (body/blickwinkel), 15 (snowflake/Jussi Pietarinen), 16 (bird/Danack), 16 (escape/Susan McWhinney), 16 (fight/David Osborn), 16 (worm/Phil Degginger), 16 (hunt/AfriPics.com), 22 (strong/Nigel Cattlin), 22 (patient/Paul Springett A), 22 (calm/Juniors Bildarchiv GmbH), 22 (fierce/Image Source), 28 (freeze/Richard Levine), 28 (melt/Image Source), 28 (heat/Martin Muransky), 28 (solid/Aflo Foto Agency), 31 (branch/PJM Images), 32 (branch/PJM Images), 33 (puddle/macana), 33 (ice cubes/Givaga), 34 (balloons/Stuart Gregory), 34 (kettle/studiomode), 34 (popcorn/Helen Sessions), 34 (icicle/Andy Selinger), 34 (candle/ Lenscap), 35 (coffee/HG Delaney), 35 (carrots/Roy LANGSTAFF), 36 (freezer/mark phillips), 36 (plastic bags/Pashkov Andrey), 36 (pour/Tony Cordoza), 36 (cream/foodfolio), 36 (salt/ClassicStock), 42 (coffee/ Bon Appetit), 42 (fruit/foodfolio), 48 (radio/studiomode), 48 (e-mail/Ian Dagnall), 48 (travel/Angela Hampton Picture Library), 48 (airplane/Antony Nettle), 48 (Internet/Ajith Achuthan), 54 (truck/David Touchtone), 54 (motorcycle/Motoring Picture Library), 56 (clerk/Image Source Plus), 56 (enter/Dan Atkin), 62 (couch/Winston Link), 62 (sink/Nikreates), 68 (test score/D. Hurst), 68 (left/Image Source), 68 (balloon/Jon Helgason), 68 (candle/Ian Dagnall), 68 (lamp/photonic 15), 74 (macaroons/Emilio Ereza), 74 (clean/Susan Norwood), 74 (dirty/Arterra Picture Library), 74 (full/Tetra Images), 76 (baker/Juice Images), 76 (bored/JJ pixs), 76 (cook/john angerson), 76 (steal/Caro), 76 (dig up/Richard Peters), 82 (baby/RubberBall), 83 (fruit/Tim Hill), 88 (lifeguard/Nick Turner), 88 (litter/Everyday Images), 88 (take turns/Cultura Creative), 89 (lifeguard/Richard Splash), 90/91 (crossing guard/Janine Wiedel Photolibrary), 90 (clean up/Blend Images), 91 (lifeguard/Richard Splash), 91 (sign/Urban Zone), 91 (zoo/ Ellen McKnight), 92 (crossing guard/Janine Wiedel Photolibrary), 94 (crossing guard/Dennis MacDonald), 94 (kitchen/paul eccleston), 94 (cafetieria/Sergio Azenha), 94 (classroom/yang yu), 94 (crosswalk/MARKA), 96 (share/Blend Images), 96 (grab/dk), 96 (put away/Bob Ebbesen), 96 (thoughtful/VStock), 96 (knock/BlueBell), 96 (rude/OJO Images Ltd), 102 (ipad/D. Hurst), 102 (laptop/ Sergio Azenha), 102 (camera/Sergio Azenha), 108 (reduce - full/Alan Gignoux), 108 (reduce- empty/ Katharine Andriotis), 108 (sunlight/Vitaliy Pakhnyushchyy), 108 (trash/Peter Alvey), 108 (wood/Tristan Leverett), 108 (resources/Aurora Photos), 110 (FORGET Patrick/SAGAPHOTO.COM), 114 (tent/Judith Collins), 114 (fish/Cultura Creative), 116 (stationary store/Eye Ubiquitous), 116 (machine/Roger Bamber), 116 (diary/Ian Dagnall), 122 (alarm clock/Denys Prokofyev), 128 (right/roger ashford), 128 (trumpet/Judith Collins), 128 (low/Lebrecht Music and Arts Photo Library), 128 (high/James Davies), 130 (singing/Blend Images), 132 (singing/Blend Images), 134 (laugh/MBI), 134 (unhappy/D. Hurst), 134 (yawn/MBI), 134 (nervous/RubberBall), 136 (solo/Blend Images), 136 (wait/mauritius images GmbH), 136 (worried/YAY Media AS), 142 (lunch/Tetra Images), 142 (concert/imagebroker), 142 (mistake/Radius Images), 148 (light/Tobias), 148 (ground/Martin Lladó//Gaia Moments), 148 (pull/PhotoAlto), 148 (movement/Nicholas Burningham), 150 (push/Ian M Butterfield [001 JBE]), 154 (mouse/Keith Leighton), 154 (suitcase/Tony Cordoza), 154 (door/Zoonar GmbH), 154 (drawer/MIXA), 156 (angry/MBI), 156 (goat/Ian Wray), 156 (stubborn/PHOVOIR), 156 (mountain/blickwinkel), 161 (man/MBI), 162 (equipment/Joe Belanger), 162 (baseball/Ilene MacDonald), 162 (golf/moodboard), 168 (collage/GLC Pix), 168 (sculpture/Alex Segre/), 168 (nature/Johner Images), 168 (spiral/YAY Media AS), 168 (star/Aydin Buyuktas), 168 (straight/All Canada Photos), 168 (window/Clearviewimages RF), 168 (sculpture head/ Johnny Jones), 171 (painting/RIA Novosti), 172 (painting/RIA Novosti), 174 (tiles/Isabelle Plasschaert), 174 (pottery/Harry Lands), 174 (sketchpad/amana images inc.), 174 (photograph/D. Hurst), 174 (origami/Akihito Yokoyama), 176 (golden/Andres Rodriguez), 176 (crumple/Andres Rodriguez), 176 (fold/YAY Media AS), 176 (shiny/Oleksiy Maksymenko), 182 (markers/FogStock), 182 (scissors/ Zoonar GmbH), 182 (glue/Tetra Images), 182 (coloured pencils/Art Directors & TRIP), 182 (markers/ Helen Sessions), 182 (markers/Helen Sessions); Ardea p.16 (pinecone/Pascal Goetgheluck); 16 (peck/ Brian Bevan), 16 (berries/M. Watson), Ben Heine pp.169 (leopard), 171 (leopard); Corbis UK Ltd pp.31 (puddle/Daniel Ammann/Reuters), 56 (visi/Steve Chenn), 102 (computer/Tetra Images), 108 (reuse/Tetra Images), 114 (surf/David Pu'u), 134 (smile/Edith Held), 148 (push/Randy Faris), 161 (boy/ Patrick Wittmann/cultura); Fotolia p.33 (soup/Jack Jelly); George W. Hart p.171 (sculpture); Getty Images pp.8 (salamander/Jasius), 8 (gills/Gail Shumway), 11 (panda/OTHK), 16 (creep/Kim Partridge/ Partridge-PetPics), 22 (smart/Cyril Ruoso/JH Editorial), 28 (liquid/_ta'_), 31 (pan/Bob Ingelhart), 36 (mixture/Dave King), 42 (tea/Zlatko Kostic), 42 (pasta/Chris Ted), 48 (letter/Steve Gorton and Karl Shone), 49 (posting letter/Topical Press Agency), 50 (posting letter/Topical Press Agency), 51 (radio/ Camerique Archive), 52 (radio/Camerique Archive), 54 (cable car (close up)/Justin Sullivan), 56 (arrive/ Ira Block), 56 (check/Lane Oatey/Blue Jean Images), 68 (take away/Image Source), 74 (tired/uwe umstÂ tter), 74 (hungry/Tomas Rodriguez), 76 (jar/Thomas Northcut), 76 (hide/JGI/Jamie Grill), 76 (greedy/ Design Pics/Dean Muz), 76 (let go/Cultura/Igore), 88 (principal/Gary Conner), 88 (crossing guard/Carline Jean/Sun Sentinel/MCT), 88 (polite/stockstudioX), 94 (living room/David Papazian), 96 (pass/sozaijiten/ Datacraft), 114 (ski/Karl Weatherly), 114 (camp/Bellurget Jean Louis), 114 (ride horse/Miodrag Gajic), 116 (rescue/altrendo images), 116 (carton/craftvision), 122 (time/Marco Marchi), 128 (wrong/Stockbyte), 128 (wolf/Mmphotos), 128 (sleepy/Christopher Hope-Fitch), 128 (feelings-sad/ULTRA.F), 128 (feelings-happy/Sam Edwards), 128 (excited/Blend Images/John Lund/Marc Romanelli), 130 (sleeping/Robert Dant), 134 (cry/by Dina Marie), 134 (proud/J and J Productions), 136 (record/Bob Ingelhart), 136 (musician/Cultura/DUEL), 136 (tears/sudo takeshi), 136 (flu/Tom Grill), 142 (singins/Redhaus Photography), 142 (fans/AFP/Getty Images), 148 (heavy/MARIUS BECKER/AFP), 148 (throw/Roberto A Sanchez), 150 (pull/Michael Hitoshi), 154 (stapler/Stockbyte), 156 (forward/Thomas Winz), 156 (horns/ GUY Christian/hemis.fr), 156 (wet/Andreas Arnold), 162 (football/Steve Debenport), 162 (tennis/ STOCK4B), 168 (spring/Savushkin), 168 (star light/Katja Kircher), 174 (paper/MamiGibbs), 174 (mobile/ Daniel Box - dbox.us), 176 (edge/Roc Canals Photography), 182 (watercolours/Andy Crawford), 182 (watercolours/Andy Crawford); Mary Evans Picture Library p.51 (stagecoach/Country Life/IPC Media Ltd/Mary); Oxford University Press pp.8 (skin/Digital Vision), 9 (g of Amazing/Digital Vision), 10 (g of Amazing/Digital Vision), 33 (tomato/Digital Vision), 48 (communication/Glowimages), 54 (boat/ Photodisc), 56 (poor/Chris Pancewicz), 56 (ask/Gareth Boden), 88 (librarian/Steve Hix), 96 (wash/ BlueMoon Stock), 108 (smoke/Radius Images), 108 (landfill/Photodisc), 116 (recycling plant/Mar Photographics), 136 (hummingbird/William Leaman), 154 (broom/Dennis Kitchen Studio, Inc.), 162 (hockey/Photodisc), 162 (basketball/Brand X Pictures), 176 (climb/Javier Pierini); Rex Features pp.28 (gas/WestEnd61), 142 (autograph/Aflo/Rex Features); shutterstock pp.8 (wings/Magnus Haese), 8 (fur/Skylines), 8 (eggs/dompr), 9 (parrot/Mircea BEZERGHEANU), 9 (A of Animals/Karen Katrjyan), 9 (a of animals/Nadezhda Bolotina), 9 (i of Animals/Mircea BEZERGHEANU), 9 (l of animals/Bairachnyi Dmitry), 9 (m of animals/Aleksandar Mijatovic), 9 (n of animals/val lawless), 9 (s of Animals/Eric Isselee), 9 (A of amazing/Perig), 9 (a of amazing/Ohmega1982), 9 (i of amazing/Michal Ninger), 9 (m of Amazing/Eric Isselee), 9 (n of amazing/Filip Fuxa), 9 (z of amazing/Karen Katrjyan), 10/11 (background/ Kletr), 10 (A of amazing/Perig), 10 (a of amazing/Ohmega1982), 10 (i of amazing/Michal Ninger), 10 (m of Amazing/Eric Isselee), 10 (n of amazing/Filip Fuxa), 10 (z of amazing/Karen Katrjyan), 10 (parrot/ Mircea BEZERGHEANU), 11 (A of Animals/Karen Katrjyan), 11 (a of animals/Nadezhda Bolotina), 11 (i of Animals/Mircea BEZERGHEANU), 11 (l of animals/Bairachnyi Dmitry), 11 (m of animals/Aleksandar Mijatovic), 11 (n of animals/val lawless), 11 (s of Animals/Eric Isselee), 13 (fur/jojof), 13 (scales/ Skynavin), 15 (birdhouse/satit_srihin), 15 (butterfly/Sari ONeal), 15 (jellyfish/bierchen), 22 (gentle/ Volodymyr Goinyk), 28 (ice/l i g h t p o e t), 28 (steam/Pat LaCroix), 28 (flow/jurra8), 33 (water/Pavlo Loushkin), 33 (juice/victoriaKh), 33 (snowman/Smit), 33 (orange/Alex Staroseltsev), 34 (ice pop/Elena Schweitzer), 34 (balloon/pukach), 36 (closed/Simon Bratt), 36 (open/Simon Bratt), 36 (sugar/Africa Studio), 42 (meal/wolfmaster13), 42 (salad/Africa Studio), 42 (vegetables/vanillaechoes), 48 (news/ RTimages), 50/51 (girl/Aaron Amat), 51 (plane/pio3), 51 (tv/dotshock), 54 (cable car/Vacclav), 54 (horse/ B747), 54 (bus/Tupungato), 56 (sick/Rob Hainer), 56 (crowded/Rafael Ramirez Lee), 62 (chair/photosync), 62 (lamp/Phiseksit), 62 (clock/Mauro Carli), 62 (bathtub/Ttatty), 74 (thirsty/3445128471), 82 (monkey/ LeonP), 88 (traffic light/Tomasz Bidermann), 94 (swimming pool/Cheryl Casey), 96 (invite/Kris Jacobs), 102 (headphones/Alexander Demyanenko), 102 (tablet/vovan), 102 (cell phone/Berislav Kovacevic), 108 (land/Kevin Eaves), 114 (hike/Markus Mainka), 116 (shelf/albund), 116 (blow/Monika Gniot), 116 (paper/Furtseff), 122 (week/vovan), 122 (nine/cromic), 129 (girl/Jacek Chabraszewski), 130/131 (girl/ Jacek Chabraszewski), 136 (notes/Andrew Gentry), 142 (interview/CarlaVanWagoner), 150/151 (background/Reinhold Leitner), 150 (girl rope/effe45), 151 (boy push/Pressmaster), 156 (compass/Garsya), 161 (baby/Ozgur Coskun), 168 (pattern/Michal Ninger), 168 (oval/Benjamin Albiach Galan), 168 (crescent/Georgios Kollidas), 168 (sunflowers/Fedorov Oleksiy), 168 (ruler/inxti), 168 (pattern/Arkady Mazor), 168 (collage/Valentina_S), 168 (moon/Albie Bredenhann), 174 (scissors/ Sergey Skleznev), 174 (camera/DeSerg), 174 (art materials/oil paints brush easel), 174 (drawing/Mike Demidov), 174 (painting/CYC), 174 (mosaic/konmesa), 176 (waves/pfshots), 176 (seal/Johan Larson), 176 (crane/Neil Bradfield), 182 (watercolours/Christopher Elwell), 182 (chalk/Diana Taliun), 182 (glue/3drenderings), 182 (scissors (yellow/green)/Vladvm), 182 (scissors (yellow/green)/Vladvm), 182 (glue/3drenderings), 182 (chalk/daffodilred), 182 (pencils/Africa Studio), 182 (scissors (yellow/ green)/Vladvm); 182 (chalk/daffodilred), Superstock Ltd. pp.8 (mammals/ Biosphoto), 88 (clean up/ Clover), 148 (speed/ Transtock), 150 (boxes/Flirt), 154 (boys/ Photononstop); Zooid Pictures p.48 (text message)

The Publishers would also like to thank the following for their kind permission to reproduce photographs and other copyright material:

Corbis pp.26 (hot spring, Iceland/Ragnar Th. Sigurdsson), 106 (Danum Valley, Borneo/Frans Lanting), 166 (making mosaic/Atlantide Phototravel); Getty Images pp.66 (boy with cherries/Fuse), 86 (girls playing/Purestock), 126 (girls playing music/Terry Vine), 146 (skiing/Adie Bush); Mary Evans Picture Library p.46 (Oxford Street); Nature Picture Library p.6 (African elephant/Pete Oxford).

Cover photo: Craig van der Lende/Getty Images

Cover illustration: Michael Slack